H. K. W. Patterson

War Memories of Fort Monroe and Vicinity

Containing an account of the memorable battle between the Merrimac

and Monitor, the incarceration of Jefferson C. Davis and other topics

H. K. W. Patterson

War Memories of Fort Monroe and Vicinity
Containing an account of the memorable battle between the Merrimac and Monitor, the incarceration of Jefferson C. Davis and other topics

ISBN/EAN: 9783337267605

Printed in Europe, USA, Canada, Australia, Japan

Cover: Foto ©ninafisch / pixelio.de

More available books at **www.hansebooks.com**

WAR MEMORIES

OF

FORT MONROE AND VICINITY

Containing an Account of the Memorable
Battle Between the Merrimac and
Monitor, the Incarceration of
Jefferson Davis, and Other
Topics of Interest Con-
cerning the Fort and
Neighborhood

— BY —

H. K. W. PATTERSON,

Sergeant Battery A, Third Artillery

Entered according to act of Congress, in the year 1885, by H. K. W. Patterson, John M. Pool, and Gottlieb Dueschle, in the office of the Librarian of Congress, at Washington D. C., April 1885.

NOTICE TO THE PUBLIC.

—:o:—

The information contained in this book concerning Hampton, National Military Home, and The Hampton Normal and Agricultural Institute, etc., which we were kindly permitted to use by Mr. C. W. Betts, Manager of the Normal School Press, was taken from his "Visitors Hand Book of Old Point Comfort and Vicinity," which is a copyrighted work.

Any publication of a similar character will be contested by him under the copyright law.

PATTERSON, POOL & DEUSCHLE,
Publishers.

DEDECATION.

——:o:——

To First Lieutenant Constantine Chase, 3rd Artillery, formerly Adjutant of the U. S. Artillery School, and under whose auspices our little work was commenced, this book is respectfully dedicated by

THE AUTHOR.

PREFACE.

———:o:———

In presenting this little work to the Public, the author has endeavored to give an answer to questions, which have been constantly asked by visitors to the Fort, concerning its extent, area, armament, and a hundred different points, which we have endeavored to elucidate.

We are indebted to several sources for our information, to all of whom we are grateful, but we wish particularly to express our appreciation of the valuable information concerning. The National Soldiers' Home, Hampton Normal and Agricultural Institute, and Hampton, gleaned from the Guide Book compiled by C. W. Betts, Esq., the gentlemanly and accommodating Manager of the Normal School Press. To him, and one other source, Lieut. Col. John H. Craven, U. S. A., the Medical attendant of Jefferson Davis, we would especially return thanks.

We send this book forth to the public; and bespeak for it a generous patronage. Should we succeed in satisfying the want it is intended to supply, its author's object will have been accomplished.

H. K. W. P.

ACROSTIC.

——:o:——

Frowningly from its buttressed walls on Chesapeake's bright crystal bay,
O'er all its mighty shadow cast, Monroe uplifts its granite form.
Reposing calmly on the shore whose sand its moated waters lave,
The stern epitome it seems of martial power and majesty.

Marred though it is by time and tide, and age its weaknesses betrays,
On its proud mien we gaze, and thought drifts backward for a score of years
'Neath cloudy sky and lowering tempest sounding loudly overhead,
Right gallantly our banner floated from its staff nor e'er was lowered;
Our country's safety guarded well at her hands suffered not a whit.
Emblem majestic, firm it stands, of power a fitting prototype.

CHAPTER I.

"Roll on, thou deep and dark blue Ocean — roll!
Ten thousand fleets sweep over thee in vain ;
Man marks the earth with ruin — his control
Stops with the shore ; — upon the watery plain
The wrecks are all thy deed, nor doth remain
A shadow of man's ravage, save his own,
When for a moment, like a drop of rain,
He sinks into thy depths with bubbling groan,
Without a grave, unknell'd uncoffin'd and unknown."

Approaches to Fort Monroe.

There are none who can appreciate these magnificent lines of Lord Byron to their fullest extent, so well, as those who have viewed in its broad expanse, the subject of the apostrophe of which our quotation is but a fragment. To thoroughly grasp the sublimity of the subject which inspired the majestic strain of this King of Poets, one must see in all its grandeur, and view in its limitless extent, the object of his lofty praise, and his inimitably painted word-pictures.

To gaze upon the "illimitable waste of waters," and contemplate Divinity through this most awe-inspiring and impressive of His Creations, conveys to the mind of the spectator a new meaning, and a truer appreciation of the majesty of Byron's conceptions, and the appropriateness with which he eulogizes this hoary-headed and crystal-crowned Monarch.

Tossing upon the heaving swell of the mighty Atlantic, or gliding upon its placid bosom serenely, when devoid of storms it seems like a magnificent mirror, from which is reflected the Almighty's face; viewing in untrammeled proportions its mighty domain, man's puny efforts seem inconceivably insignificant. There is no sight which impresses one more forcibly with a sense of his own littleness, as to be abroad on the "rolling deep," and have naught to intercept his limit of vision save the "watery plain," and the boundless horizon.

Sights which rivet the attention of the traveler, and excite his interest, meet his eye as he is being swept northward by the Atlantic's restless tide. Many mighty estuaries, almost oceans in themselves, loom up before him, and impress him, first with their magnitude, and secondly with their importance commercially.

The first which meets his eye, and impresses him with its magnificence, and importance as a mercantile highway, and the basins of whose tremendous feeding streams take in a scope of territory unequalled in extent, and drain a country unsurpassed for beauty and variety of climate, temperture and productions, is the Gulf of Mexico. Its tropical-fringed shores luxuriating in a growth of vegetation, and blooming with a variety and splendor of verdure, seen only under the burning suns and torrid skies of the Tropics, present a picture to the eye of the spectator, viewing it for the first time, never to be forgotten, and one which impresses him with a renewed sense of the extent and magnificence of our own beloved country. Here may be seen in all their beauty and perfection those rare and delicate fruits and exotics, which are such an important element in the festivity and ornamentation of more northern climes, and less favored localities, and which prove such a rarity to those fortunate enough to possess them.

The second arm of the Atlantic which presents itself to the view of the traveler, and swells with its mighty volume, its ever onward rolling tide, is the Chesapeake Bay. It is the largest on the eastern coast of the United States, being 200 miles long, and from 4 to 40 broad. This magnificent inland sea has to do more intimately with our subject, and will,

eventually, bring us to the objective point of our journey.
Branching off from the Ocean, with a width at its mouth of 12 miles, it is difficult to tell where the one ends, and the other begins. Guarded at its mouth by two royal sentinels, Chesapeake's tide travels oceanward, and affords an outlet for both Maryland's and Virginia's manufacturing interests.

On the North side is Cape Charles in Latitude 37° 3' North, and Longitude 76° 2' West; and on the South Cape Henry, in Latitude 36° 35' North, and Longitude 76° 4' West. Both these promontories are in Virginia. These two capes, named after the sons of King James, stand guard over one of the finest bays in the world, whose importance, commercially, can only be properly estimated by those indebted to it as a medium of traffic.

Chesapeake Bay has numerous arms, which receive many navigable rivers, such as, the Susquehanna and the Patapsco on the north, through Maryland, and the James, on the southwest, from Virginia. The Potomac on the west, flowing between these two states, also empties its waters into the same reservoir. The country drained by these large tributaries, will ever remain prominent in American History, as having been the theatre of some of the most fiercely contested battles of the War of the Rebellion, and the Potomac river, especially, giving name to one of the strongest forces which the Federal Government had at its command, viz., the "Army of the Potomac," will always awaken interest in the breast of every one conversant with Columbia's history, and bring back to the minds of thousands of her sons, memories of the terrible ordeals through which she, as well as they, was compelled to pass.

Entering the Chesapeake, and sailing northward on its placid bosom for a distance of 18 or 20 miles, we reach what is known as Hampton Roads, a name familiar to all mariners, as being a synonym for rest and quiet, and a sure haven of peace and security. Here may be seen, when the "rude sons of Boreas" assert their wild dominion, and lash into mad fury the waters of the Atlantic till they seem like a boiling cauldron, scores of fishing smacks, white winged coasting schooners, and frequently, men-of-war, lying at anchor, and biding the time when the Storm King shall have been driven forth by gentle westerly breezes, whose milder domain shall again woo them forth, and tempt them on their voyage oceanward.

It sets in westward from Chesapeake Bay, and its narrow entrance is guarded by Fort Monroe. Not far from the entrance it spreads out into an oval habor five miles in diameter. Here and there, is a shallow place, but almost every part is deep enough to float the largest vessel. The estuaries of two rivers enter the top of the habor from opposite directions: the James, from the northwest, and the Elizabeth, from the southeast. It lays between Hampton and Norfolk, Virginia, and forms the entrance to the James river. Its depth ranges from 5 to 7 fathoms. The Fort commanding the entrance to the Roads, is situated on a point of land on the north shore near its mouth. At the head of the estuary of the Elizabeth, 8 miles from its opening, are Norfolk, on the east side, and Portsmouth, with Gosport, its suburb, on the west. At the latter point, there is a U. S. Navy Yard, 20 miles from the entrance of the Roads.

The interest of these waters historically, began early in the history of America, they having sheltered as early as 1608, Captain John Smith and a party of companions, from destruction by tempest, while exploring the shores of the Chesapeake who, after being exposed to the full fury of the blast, sought a convenient habor. York and James rivers were passed, but, owing to the storm, they could not make them. They finally came to the sandy tongue of land which projects into the entrance of the James river, which, having rounded, they found security and shelter. Out of gratitude for their deliverance, and most appropriately selecting a name for this locality, they called it *Point Comfort*. The adjective *old*, has since been added, to distinguish this harbor and vicinity, from one of a similar character higher up the bay, called New Point Comfort.

Coming down to a later period in our country's history, we again see this same peaceful harbor proudly giving anchorage and shelter to the French fleet, which proved such an invaluable auxiliary to Washington's forces in the subjugation of Yorktown, and here also at a later period, in 1813, the British fleet retired and found shelter, while in small boats their troops landed, and carried havoc and destruction into the quiet village of Hampton. Still further on in the annals of our Nation, we see these same waters figuring prominently in the War which deluged our land with blood for four long years, from 1861–1865.

Here rendezvoused the fleet and transports accompanying the "Burnside Expedition," which in a little over three months, succeeding, in conjunction with the land forces, in capturing and restoring to the Union from which they had been foully and ungratefully taken by the Confederate Government, all the important points on the coast of North Carolina.

Thus it will be seen that these waters are classic in American history. From the time they afforded protection to Captain John Smith, with his three ships in the seventeenth century, before the birth of the American Republic, until over 250 years later in 1861–65, witnessing the most fearful and stupendous warfare of modern times, it has been the theatre of many important scenes; in the latter struggle especially, owing to its proximity to our great Navy Yard at Norfolk. But, towering far above them all, the glorious fight between the "Monitor," on the Union side, and the "Merrimac" on the Confederate side, (the latter vessel having been re-baptized the "Virginia," by the Confederates), most commands our admiration, as being of the greatest importance, not only in the affairs of this country, but to the world at large.

Previous to the recountal of the battle a brief account of the two vessels, their origin, inventors, and builders, will form a fitting prelude.

The Confederate authorities early saw the necessity of floating batteries to defend their coasts, harbors, and inland waters. They could not hope to rival their enemy in the number of vessels. They must rely on the superiority of a few. To construct iron-clads required months of time, and a large amount of capital, neither of which the Confederate Government possessed. They had no means of building a hull or making an engine. But imbecility, treachery, and accident, gave them a hull and engine ready for use.

In 1855, the United States built, at different navy yards, three powerful steam frigates, the "Merrimac," the "Roanoke," and the "Minnesota." They were nearly all alike of about 3500 tuns burden, carrying from forty to fifty guns. In April, 1861, the "Merrimac" was at the Norfolk Navy Yard, undergoing repairs. When that place was abandoned, she was set on fire, scuttled and sunk. She was soon after raised by the Confederates, and a Committee was ordered to examine into her condition, and the use to which she might be put. They reported that her upper works were so much damaged that she could not be rebuilt without great expense and delay; but the bottom part of the hull, the boilers, and heavy parts of the engine, were almost without injury, and that these could be adapted for a shot-proof steam battery more quickly and for one third of the sum, which it would cost to construct such a vessel anew.

The plan was furnished by Brooks and Porter. The central part of the hull for something more than half its length, was cut down to within three or four feet of the water-line to form the gun-deck, and the hull was plated with iron to a depth of about six feet below the water-line. A casemate of novel construction was built on the gun-deck. Pine beams, a foot square and fifteen feet long, were placed side by side, like rafters, at an inclination of about 45 degrees. These projected over the sides of the vessel like the eaves of a house, their ends dipping two feet below the water. Upon these beams were placed two layers of oak planks four inches thick : one layer horizontal, and the other vertical. This was first overlaid with ordinary flat bars of iron four and a half inches thick. Experiments showed that this thickness of iron was inadequate, and a layer of railroad iron was added. This casemate did not come to a point, like the roof of a house, but there was a flat space on the top, rendered bomb-proof by plates of wrought iron. From this roof projected a short smoke-stack.

The armament consisted of eight 11-inch guns, four on each side, and a 100-pound rifled Armstrong gun at each end. The ends of the vessel were cut down still lower, so as to be two feet below water. A light bulwark, or false bow, of wood was built. This served the two-fold purpose of preventing the water from banking up against the case-mate when the vessel was in motion, and of a tank to diminish the draft. To this craft was given the name of the " Virginia." The draft of the "Merrimac" had been about twenty-three feet, and her speed was fourteen or fifteen miles an hour, after her conversion into an iron clad, she drew twenty-five feet of water, and her speed was reduced to seven knots and a- half.

Some time elapsed before the Federal Government perceived the absolute necessity of iron clad vessels. Experiments had been made by the Stevens' Brothers of New Jersey, in the construction of an iron battery upon an original plan, and Congress, at length, on the 3rd of August, 1862, appropriated $1,500,000 for the building of iron-clads. The proposals were sent out, and the Commission reported in favor of three different vessels. The "Ironsides" by Merrick and Sons of Philadelphia, a regular man-of-war, 20 guns, and covered with $4\frac{1}{2}$ inches of solid plate. The "Galena" by C. S. Bushnell, of New Haven, a steamer, brigantine rigged, 18 guns, plated with from 2 to 4 inches of thin rolled iron. The third was an anomaly in naval architecture, with John Ericsson of New York for its inventor.

"John Ericsson was born in the Province of Vermland, in Sweden, on July 31st, 1803. He was a Swedish Engineer of prominence. He received several titles and dignities both in this country and in Europe, receiving the distinction of L. L. D. from an American University.

He came to America in 1839, landing at New York, Nov. 23rd. Some time previous to 1854, he had been revolving in his mind the idea of an iron-plated shot-proof ship of war. On September 26th 1854, plans and specifications of the "Monitor," as she afterwards appeared, were sent from New York to the Emperor Napoleon III, thus giving him an opportunity of monopolizing for the French Nation in the Crimean War, this new departure in naval warfare. The Emperor at once acknowledged Ericsson's letter, but, fortunately for America the offer was not accepted, and the "Monitor" was first used for the protection of his adopted country.

Following will be found a copy of a letter explaining why Ericsson called his ship the "Monitor."

(Copy)
NEW YORK, January 20th, 1862.

Sir: —

In accordance with your request, I now submit for your approbation a name for the the floating battery at Green Point.

The impregnable and aggressive character of this structure will admonish the leaders of the Southern Rebellion that the batteries on the banks of their rivers will no longer present barriers to the entrance of the Union forces.

The iron-clad intruder will thus prove a severe monitor to those leaders. But there are other leaders who will also be startled and admonished by the booming of the guns from the impregnable iron turret. "Downing Street" will hardly view with indifference this last "Yankee notion," this monitor. To the Lords of Admiralty the new craft will be a monitor, suggesting doubts as to the propriety of completing those four steel-clad vessels at three-and-a-half millions apiece.

On these and many similar grounds I propose to name the new battery "Monitor."

Your obedient servant,

J. ERRICSSON.

To Gustavus V. Fox,
Assistant Secretary of the Navy:

Having thus given a preliminary look at the inventor, we will now look at the ship itself.

Her dimensions were as follows: = Extreme length 172 feet, this included her armor, and also that part which extended beyond the hull proper. The length of the hull proper was 124 feet: Her total beam 41 ⅓ feet, including over armor and backing; beams of her hull proper 34 feet; her depth 11 feet; draught 10 feet; her total weight with everything on board was 900 tons; the diameter of her turret inside was 20 feet; its height 9 feet; its thickness 8 inches; the vessel's armor, 5 inches of iron and 5 feet of oak.

Her shape was that of half of an egg-shell, slightly flattened at the bottom. Five feet below the top there was an iron shelf projecting nearly four feet from the sides. This was filled with oaken blocks, over which were bolted five series of iron plates each an inch thick. This armor shelf or platform projected 16 feet at the stern, in order to cover the rudder, and propeller, and ten feet at the bow to protect the anchor. Her armament consisted of two 11-inch guns.

The principal feature of the "Monitor," of course, was her revolving turret. It was constructed of plates of iron an inch thick, three feet wide, and nine feet in length. Eight of these plates constituted its thickness. It was thus nine feet high and eight inches thick, with a diameter of twenty feet. The two port-holes were of an oval shape just large enough to allow the guns to be elevated to secure the proper range. It was made to revolve upon a central shaft by means of a separate engine. Therefore when she presented herself her deck was a smooth surface, broken only by the huge round turret, and a low square pilot-house near the bow.

It is not much of a matter of wonderment that she should be termed a "cheese-box," by her confederate opponents. Her propelling power was in her stern.

A few weeks later than the time of her completion was to be fought a naval battle not only between the first iron-clads, but the first between screw-propelled ships.

By a singular coincidence both the "Merrimac" and the "Monitor" were finished on the 5th of March, 1862. On the 4th of March, Lieut. Commander John L. Worden, received orders to proceed with his vessel to Hampton Roads, and report to the senior Naval Officer there. This in perfect ignorance of the mighty results to follow. The " Monitor " left the Lower Bay of New York on the afternoon of the 6th of March, 1862. passing Cape Henry light-house March 8th, 1862. This day, one of the saddest of the Rebellion, had witnessed the detruction of the U. S. ships "Cumberland" and "Congress," by the rebel ram "Merrimac." For weeks previous to her arrival conflicting reports had reached Fort Monroe, and vicinity, of the intentions and movement of this dreaded monster. All were on the *qui vive*, anticipating her arrival, but dreading the consequences.

At noon on Saturday March the 8th, the "Merrimac" rounded Sewell's Point, standing up towards Newport News. She was attended by the "Frazer" and "Yorktown," two small steamers armed with rifled guns. She was commanded by Franklin Buchanan, who had entered the United States Navy thirty-five years before. He stood high on the roll having attained the rank of Captain. He was commander of the Navy Yard at Washington when the war broke out. He, resigned his commission, and entered heart and hand into the Confederate service. Having been born in Maryland, he could not even plead having followed his native state in taking up arms against his country. This was the trial trip of the "Merrimac," and what throws around this contest such an extraordinary interest, is the fact that the armament and style of both ships were entirely new, and the battle was naught but a test of the powers of the two antagonists. The " Congress " and "Cumberland" were anchored off Newport News, about a quarter of a mile apart, and about the same distance from shore, the rest of the fleet were lying near Fort Monroe, six miles distant. As soon as the "Merrimac" came within range of the "Congress," she opened fire upon her with her 100-pound bow gun. The heartlessness and cruelty of this warfare can be slightly estimated when it is taken into consideration that the favorite brother of Captain Buchanan was purser on board of the "Congress," and when he gave the order to fire, he knew he was aiming his missiles against his brother's life. The attack was made at dead slack water, the commander of the "Merrimac" knowing that his two opponents being sailing ships could not use springs on their cables at that time to present their broadsides to the enemy. The "Congress" answered the attack of her powerful antagonist with a whole broadside from eleven 9-inch Dahlgrens. They rebounded from her iron sides, inflicting no more damage, than if they had been pebbles. The "Merrimac" seemed to be anxious to test her defenses, and they justified the belief in her impregnability. Six broadsides were delivered without any essential damage. She kept straight on until her bow pointed straight at the "Cumberland." This was at three o'clock in the afternoon.

The huge monster opened fire upon the ill-fated vessel, at the same time striking her with her iron beak, at a terrific momentum, below the water-line, making a ragged opening large enough to admit the body of a man. The "Merrimac" then opened fire. Broadside after broadside was delivered in rapid succession, each shot reaching a vital part. Some idea of the destructiveness of the fire may be imagined from the fact that the first shot killed and wounded ten men at the after pivot gun. The second shot killed and wounded twelve men at the forward pivot gun. The following statement made by an officer on board the "Cumberland," and taken from "The First Monitor," a paper read before the Buffalo Historical Society by Eben P. Dorr. gives a graphic account of the heart-rending scenes happening in connection with this terrible conflict.

Just after the ramming of the "Cumberland" he says:—"I was looking through the air port of the sick bay, at the time and had a full view of the "Merrimac." She was like a large iron shed sunk down to the roof, with a gun put in the gable. The shock was tremendous. I heard the stones rattling in the gunner's room underneath, and some of the bolts in the hanging knees were driven in, and the water spouted in, in a full stream. Part of the wounded had been brought down and were partially dressed, when a percussion shell came through the spar deck hatch, bursting in the sick bay immediately under the spar deck, killing four of the wounded men. By this time the ship was settling by the head, and we moved to the steerage. It was necessary to lift the wounded, brought down to the berth deck, on to the big racks and mess-chests, to save them from drowning in the water which was flowing in very fast.

"All this time, the three rebel ships continued to fire on us, and it was returned as warmly. Trunks of cartridges were hoisted on the gun deck and opened, the guns' crews kicked off their shoes stripped to their pants, their heads tied up with their black neck handkerchiefs, loaded, fired, yelled, and dragged the killed and wounded, amidships. There was no time for form or to send them below.

"In forty-five minutes from the time she was struck, the order was given to leave quarters and save themselves as best they could. The ship in sinking keeled over. The ladders were almost perpendicular. The crash was fearful. As there is often in the gravest scenes a corner for the ludicrous, so there was in this. The marine drummer holding on to his drum, the men pushing him up from below, landing him on deck with it, caused a laugh at his expense, desperately as we were situated.

"When the spar deck was reached, it inclined like the roof

of a house. The boats previous to the action, had all been lowered and made fast in a line on the shore side. Every one took to the water and swam for the boats. While hesitating at the after pivot port, a man next to me said, 'Jump! here comes the pivot gun!' It had been pivoted on the upper side, and breaking away rushed down in the water catching, as it went, Quartermaster Murray, a young, active, unwounded man. He fell, and the gun bounded on his back, like some fierce animal, breaking his spine. His face rose with an unutterable look of agony, which once seen, could never be forgotten.

The ship sunk to her tops, in which many of the men took refuge. As the boats made for the shore, the enemy continued to shell us, but we were below in the water, so that the shell went over us. One of them knocked to pieces the end of the wharf we were making for. (This is what is now known as the Baltimore Wharf, at Fort Monroe.) On landing, the soldiers met us in crowds; they hugged and embraced us, and whiskey flasks were held to our mouths, plugs of tobacco shoved into our pockets, and they cried and cheered and cursed; and we were clothed and comforted by them.

"The "Cumberland" lost one hundred and seventeen out of three hundred. Fourteen of the wounded were saved. When the order was given to leave the ships, the wounded men, most of them mangled by shell, begged to be killed rather than be left to drown, and the yell of agony as she sank was heard in the camp of the troops on shore. But *she sunk with her colors flying!* The last gun was fired by a volunteer officer, Lieutenant Randall, now in the naval service. Lieut. Morris was hailed by Captain Buchanan of the "Merrimac," 'Do you surrender?' He answered, 'No, sir!'

"The slaughter was terrible among the marines. They were commanded by Lieutenant Heywood, a gallant man.

There were many interesting scenes on board. A man dreadfully, hopelessly wounded, had been carried down to the cock-pit. While therein, his 'chummy,' or friend, with a wounded hand only, came to have it dressed, intending to return. The wounded man said, 'Tom, are you going to leave me?' Tom said, 'No, I will not!' and sat down on deck, took his friend's head in his lap, and went down with him. The cock-pit sentry also went down at his post.

"Leaving the "Cumberland," the ram went for the "Congress." She was aground and helpless. Hot shot were fired into her, and she was soon on fire. Full of wounded men, Lieutenant Smith killed, the ship on fire, the colors were hauled down at four o'clock."

The father of the commander of the "Congress" was watching the battle from the ramparts of Fort Monroe; he had been looking through his glass, and when, for a moment, he turned away, and some one else took the glass, and cried out hastily. "The "Congress" has struck her colors!" "Then," said he. "Joe is dead!" This showed the unbounded confidence felt in him by his father. To resume the thread of our story.

"A small tender from the "Merrimac," went between the "Congress" and the shore, but the Zouaves under Colonel Lozier with their rifles picked off the men in the tug, and she left without making a prisoner or securing the *flag* of the "Congress;" and then, to the surprise of every one, the "Merrimac" steamed back for Norfolk. She had left her ram in the "Cumberland," and was leaking badly. All the wounded of the "Congress" were taken ashore, and at 12:30 she blew up, the fire having reached her magazines.

An old man, Russel, aged sixty, stationed in the after magazine of the "Cumberland," went down with the ship, made his way up through the hatches, to the surface and was hauled into the mizzentop, the only one out of water. The weight rushing forward kept her head lower than the stern, entirely submerging her fore and main tops. As soon as Radford heard the firing he attempted to reach us; but the "Roanoke" was repairing her machinery, the "Minnesota" aground, and as we landed at Newport News, he rode down to the beach on a horse without saddle or bridle, merely a halter. He was ragged and muddy from falls, haggard with anxiety and regret; but brightened up when he was pointed to the flag still flying from his ship. He was noted for complete control of himself, but he cried like a child when contemplating the sad scene before him. A kinder and braver Captain never commanded a ship, and though he regretted his own absence, he approved the acts of the gallant Morris, his officers and crew, by saying: 'It could not have been done better.' For weeks after the battle, the flag of the "Cumberland" waved above her wreck, a sad, but glorious memorial of the matchless prowess and martyrdom of her crew. Thus ends the account of an eye-witness of one of the most memorable conflicts of the war. The sad fate of the "Cumberland" and "Congress" has since become the subject of song and story. The pages of history fail to record a more desperate or more gloriously contested struggle, in the annals of war.

And now, with the "Cumberland" sunk in the depths of the waters she had so gallantly tried to defend, and the wreck of the "Congress" a prey to the flames, the "Merrimac" turned her attention to the remainder of the Union fleet, and essayed to visit upon them the same fate as she had inflicted upon their unfortunate companions. The "Minnesota," which in endeavoring to go to the rescue of the "Congress" and "Cumberland" had run aground at Sewell's Point, seemed to offer an easy victory. The "Roanoke" and the "St. Lawrence," also met with the same fate.

The greater draught of the "Merrimac" prevented her

from approaching nearer than a mile to the "Minnesota" She opened fire upon this vessel, but only one shot was effective. This ineffectual contest was carried on for about two hours. The two smaller antagonists attending the "Merrimac" were soon silenced by the Dahlgren howitzers of the Federal gunboats, and the "Goliah" of the fleet unable to consummate her vicious intentions, steamed back with her consort to the protection of the batteries at the mouth of the Elizabeth. Thus ended a sad day for the anxious hearts at Old Point. All awaited with dread foreboding the rising of the morrow's sun.

This was the situation on Saturday night when the "Monitor" arrived at Hampton Roads, having left New York Bay two days before. Some time previous to her arrival in the Roads, the sound of the sanguinary conflict had reached her, and shells were seen to burst in the air. The disappointed officers on board the "Monitor" were sadly chagrined, supposing the report to proceed from an attack on Norfolk, for which they had arrived too late. They urged their ship on as rapidly as possible, and a pilot was taken on board, who, terror-stricken with the frightful message he carried, told the receding day's doings in Hampton Roads. He received orders to put the "Monitor" in the neighborhood of the "Merrimac." This gave him such a fright that when he came to where his boat was anchored he quickly got aboard of her and disappeared. She however anchored alongside of the "Minnesota" a little after midnight. They anxiously awaited the dawning of the 9th of March. At about 8 o'clock in the morning the "Merrimac" was seen slowly approaching the scene of her former day's triumph.

At about the same time from the deck of the "Merrimac" the "Confederate outlook" reported a steam-tug playing round the "Minnesota." Then as the "Monitor" shot out from the lee of the "Minnesota" the news travelled along the deck like wild-fire: "Ericsson's Battery has arrived. The

Monitor has come." The pigmy size of the "Monitor," occasioned a great laugh on board the "Merrimac." They seemed disposed to treat her with contempt, and looking at the respective dimensions of the two vessels there seemed, reason for it. They had been looking for her for days.

The two antagonists slowly approached each other. When the "Merrimac" came within sight her smoke-stack was discovered to have been greased with tallow to assist in glancing the shots. As the "Monitor" came alongside of her mighty foe, she opened upon her, receiving in return broad-side after broad-side, of those death-dealing missiles, which had carried such death and desolation on board of her victims the day before, but she saw them glide from the sides of the "Monitor," like grains of sand. Then the word was passed " the Yankee cheese-box is made of iron." In the previous day's contest the "Merrimac," having lost her beak from failing to reverse her engines in time she had leaked slightly. When she had retired the preceding day, she calked up the leak as best she might, and tacked over it three or four thicknesses of canvass. Every shot fired by the " Monitor," was followed by the vessel herself, and she would drive with all the force she was able to summon from her engines, full against the "Merrimac," increasing the leak, and stripping off the iron plating from her sides with every shot. Each collision was followed by the speedy gliding of the " Monitor" in front of her foe, she being, from her smaller size, much more easily manipulated. It was the intention of Lieutenant Worden, if possible, to injure the propeller of the "Merrimac," but she missed it by a few feet.

The vessels, during the contest, were but a short distance from each other, many times their iron casings coming in contact. Broadside after broadside was delivered at this incredible short range, but the revolving turret receiving the shots at a very acute angle was simply dented. Then from the mouths of the death-dealing Dahlgren's (to ordinary ships) would belch forth their terrible response, and send thundering against the sides of her formidable adversary, the full fury of their vengeance. The armament of the "Merrimac" was extremely powerful, for the days in which it was manufactured, but often they sent their missiles only to have them broken after striking and collected as trophies from the deck of the "Monitor". This being little more than a test of the capabilities of the two vessels. their armament never having been tried, and their crews being so excited and so little used to their weapons, the guns in the first part of the contest were too highly elevated. and many of the projectiles were wasted in the air; but later in the fight the mistake was discovered, and the guns lowered. and then it was that shots from the Monitor's guns, hitting the junction formed by the meeting of the casemate and the side of the ship, caused a leak in the "Merrimac." In the early part of the contest, considerable anxiety was felt by Lieutenant Worden, as to the workings of the turret, it having been predicted that a shot striking it with great initial velocity, would so derange it as to interfere with its effective working. but having been twice struck, his confidence in his little giant. was thoroughly restored, and he renewed the contest with a great deal of zeal.

Captain Buchanan having been wounded, the command of the "Merrimac," devolved upon Captain Jones, who, remembering the terrible execution effected by her beak the day before. steers her directly against the "Monitor" with the same intention, but he "reckoned without his host," for, by a clever shift of the helm at the critical moment, giving a broad sheer with her bow towards the enemy's stern, by this means avoiding a direct blow, and receiving it at a very acute angle on the starboard quarter, it glanced off, inflicting little or no injury to the "Monitor."

The contest continued for about four hours, with the exception of an interval of fifteen minutes, when the "Monitor" hauled off to remedy some deficiency in the supply of shots in the turret, until near noon, when, being within ten yards of the enemy a shell from the "Merrimac" struck her pilot house, near the look-out hole, through which Lieut. Worden was looking. He and his Quartermaster were both looking at the time, through a slight aperture or "conning-hole," consisting of a slit between the bars, and the Quartermaster seeing the "Merrimac's" gunners sighting their gun on the the pilot-house, dropping his head at the same time gave a warning cry. But simultaneously with his warning the shell struck the opening. It exploded, fracturing one of the iron logs of which it was composed, filling Lieut. Worden's face and eyes with powder, utterly blinding and partially stunning him. His escape from death was marvellous. The top of the pilot-house was partially lifted off by the force of the concussion, which let in a flood of light so strong as to be apparent to Worden, blind as he was, and caused him to believe that the pilot-house was seriously disabled. He gave orders that Lieut. Greene should be sent for, and told him to take command. When Worden retired word was brought to him that the "Merrimac" was retiring to Norfolk. It is interesting to note that the steward of the "Merrimac," J. B. Jones is at present Light-House Keeper on the Point.

About the same time the "Monitor's" turret was struck, a shot from her had pierced the "Merrimac" near the water line, and caused a leak, and the mighty monster, despairing of overcoming her antagonist steered to Norfolk.

Thus ends the account of the most remarkable naval conflict of modern times, first because, both armament and vessels were untried, secondly the contest was between iron-clads, and the first also between screw-propellers. The end of both vessels was violent, the " Merrimac " being destroyed by the Confederates a little over a month after the battle, May 11th 1862, they being unable to take her up James River, and the " Monitor " being lost off Cape Hatteras, eleven months from the time she was launched.

Owing to the heavy armament of both vessels, it was wondered why the conflict was not more quickly settled. Mr. Newton the Chief Engineer of the " Monitor, " when questioned by the War Committee on the subject thus answered:— " It was due to the fact that the power and endurance of the 11-inch Dahlgren gun, with which the Monitor was armed were not known at the time of the battle ; hence the commander would hardly have been justified in increasing the charge of powder above that authorized in the Ordnance Manual. Subsequent experiments developed the important fact that these guns could be fired with thirty pounds of cannon powder, with solid shot. If this had been known at the time of the action. I am clearly of the opinion, that, from the close quarters at which Lieutenant Worden fought his vessel. the enemy would have been forced to surrender. It will of course, be admitted by every one, that if but a single 15-inch gun could possibly have been mounted within the turret (it was planned to carry the heaviest ordnance), the action would have been as short and decisive as the combat between the monitor Weehawken, Captain John Rodgers, and the rebel iron-clad " Atlanta, " which, in several respects was superior to the " Merrimac. " He added, that, as it was, but for the injury received by Lieutenant Worden, that vigorous officer would very likely have " badgered " the " Merrimac " to a surrender.

Soon the news was enthusiastically flashed along the telegraph wires, and the enthusiasm was as great as had been the depression, the day before. Thanks and laudations from all quarters were poured in upon the "Monitor," Ericsson, her inventor, Worden, her commander, Green, her executive officer, Newton her Chief Engineer, Stimers the Engineer detailed to accompany and report on her, and who worked the turret, all the officers in short and all the crew shared the honors. All the dignitaries of the Nation from the President down, diplomatic corps, Officers of both services, and ladies by scores, came in crowds, to see this new engine of warfare and view the site of the memorable conflict in Hampton Roads. The President having convened a Cabinet meeting, heard accidentally that Lieutenant Worden was in the city. He immediately dissolved the meeting and went to the Hotel to see him. Worden lay on the sofa blindfolded, and when Mr. Lincoln came into the parlor, he wrung his hand while the tears coursed rapidly down his cheeks. Mr. Lincoln said, "Lieutenant Worden I am honored." To which Worden replied "No, it is I who am honored."

Having thus far conducted our readers we will next discuss the surroundings of Fort Monroe.

CHAPTER II.

*Breathing of the mystic Past,
Whose mem'ries pregnant with Renown,
Carry us backward to the scenes,
Which make our Country's history;
Monroe's surroundings big with Fame,
Speak from the shades of other years,
And tell us stories, which command
From all, respect and reverence.*

SURROUNDINGS OF FORT MONROE.

Having entered the Roads, the first object which meets the eye of the observer and looms up prominently before him, is an unfinished fortification, called the "Rip-Raps." The signification of the term, and its applicability, may not be familiar, and is, therefore, deemed worthy of explanation. The term " rip-rap" is a technicality, which literally signifies, "rough stone-work," and is applied in the present instance, first, from the manner in which the foundation of the Fort was made, and, secondly, because the stones of which the walls are formed, are termed, "roughly dressed" stone.

This structure was begun sometime about the year 1821, and the foundation was made, by throwing upon the sandbar, upon which it rests, thousands of tons of stone, brought principally from Maine, some from Port Deposit, near Philadelphia, and several other places, until a groundwork of sufficient strength was obtained, upon which the present fortification was built.

Some idea of the magnitude of the work may be formed, when it is noted, that the work of forming this foundation, was an undertaking of twenty years duration. Work upon the walls was commenced about the year 1861, but previous to its inauguration, a weight of stones, exceeding by far the weight of the anticipated fortification, was placed upon the foundation to settle it firmly in its place, and thus prevent, a sinking of the structure, after its completion. The idea which popularly prevails upon the Point and its vicinity, that this place was abandoned on account of a continued sinking, is, therefore erroneous. The reason why its completion was postponed, was owing to the fact, that the Engineer having the work in charge found that the improved Ordnance of modern warfare, would speedily reduce it, and, therefore, its practical utility, if finished in consistency with the plans and specifications, was to be doubted. The same authority, however, maintains it as his opinion, that if the space between the foundation above water level, and the walls proper, was filled up with banks of sand, and armament placed upon it, as it now stands, in six months, it could be made impregnable. The work of construction was carried on for about six years, until 1867, when it ceased, and has not since been renewed.

The name of the Fort was originally, Fort Calhoun, but at the breaking out of the War of the Rebellion, owing to the views sustained by Governor John C. Calhoun, of South Carolina, after whom it was called, and, also, because he was the father of the "Repudiation" doctrine, it was changed to " Fort Wool," in honor of General Wool, whose war record was very creditable, and who at the time, was commanding the Department, embracing the same within its limits. The name " Rip-Raps, " is, however, more generally applied to it, than any other. During the War the houses now to be found upon it, were used as a prison for military convicts, who were sent to assist in the erection of " Monroe." Fort Wool was also used as a place of incarceration for rebel prisoners, during the War, and from its walls one was hung as a spy during the Rebellion.

Having viewed this curiosity until satisfied, we will next land on the Point at the Baltimore Wharf, as it is called, on account of its being more largely used by the Baltimore line of Steamers, than any other; it was built, because the "Light House Wharf," as it is generally termed, was not large enough to accommodate the shipping of freight and stores to the Point which was particularly great during the War. Since its first erection, additions have been made to it, until it has assumed its present proportions.

Having fairly landed, we are welcomed by the urbane and gentlemanly proprietor of the Hygeia Hotel, the pride of the Point, whose massive form rears itself immediately in front of us. In 1863, the present mammoth building was of very small dimensions, and was owned by a firm named Clark and Wilson, from whom it was procured by its present proprietor, Harrison Phœbus Esq. From its humble commencement, it has gradually improved, in appearance and size, until, at the present time, it stands one of the principal summer resorts on the Atlantic sea-board.

It is situated one hundred yards from Fort Monroe, at the confluence of Chesapeake Bay and Hampton Roads, about 180 miles south from Baltimore, and 15 miles north of Norfolk and Portsmouth.

The place is reached by the splendid steamers of the Bay Line, Potomac and James River Companies, running daily between Baltimore, Washington, Richmond and Norfolk, and by rail direct from Richmond via Chesapeake and Ohio Railway. These means of transit, to and fro, render the Point easy of access, and conduce to its popularity.

The Hotel is four stories in height, substantially built, and comfortably furnished; as a resort for the pleasure seeker, invalid, or resting place for tourists on their way to Florida or the North, this place is unsurpassed as a seaside resort.

Wending our way slowly along the Beach, or promenading the corridors of the Hotel, we notice the Light House, which stands prominently in view, in front of us. This Light built in 1834, shines out upon Chesapeake's gloomy waters, when storm-cloud, and temptest-shadow darken their crystal beauty and warn the storm-tossed mariner of the presence of danger. We also see, in its vicinity, the abutments standing, upon which was built a Wharf, which was used for passenger and freight traffic, until the more ample and convenient accommodations of the Baltimore Wharf superseded it. This Wharf, built in 1862 and enlarged in 1864, was first constructed on account of the Goods landing on the "Light House Wharf," having to be transported by labored pulling up a tough sandy Beach, and, also, on account of its small size, it was unable to accommodate the large amount of traffic carried on. It was built in 1882, and has since been used for the landing and shipping of heavy Ordnance.

Retracing our steps, until we again stand upon the Point, we see the Quartermaster's residence, opposite the Hotel, built in 1865, and a twin structure of the Hotel, of which it was a fac-simile. Next we have Adams Express Office built in 1873, and the large and accommodating establishment of William H. Kimberly, built in 1868. Opposite this store, and on the same side of the road, we next see confronting us, what is familiarly known as the "Gun-yard."

Embracing within its limits an area of about half an acre, it is surrounded on all sides by an iron fence, which, on first sight, presents to the eye a peculiar appearance, but, upon a closer observation, the barrels and bayonets of old-time muskets, are found to form its structure. The idea popularly prevailing on the Point, that these were trophies conquered from the Confederates during the late War, is an erroneous one. They are arms which were rendered useless in the fire at the

Washington Arsenal, in 1866, and were sent to the Point, to be put under the trip-hammer, and assist in the manufacture of other munitions of war. But the authorities having the matter in charge, conceived the idea of a different use for them. and they were placed in their present position.

They form an appropriate enclosure to contain the relics of Revolutionary times, to be found just inside the gates, which were conquered from the British at the battle of Yorktown in 1781 ; both six and twelve pounders, the former of which is now obsolete, so far as its use is concerned, in modern warfare; and other specimens of War's dread array.

Twenty odd years ago, the ground covered by the Yard's present dimensions, was more than one third ruled over and submerged beneath the waters of Chesapeake Bay. A wharf ran from where the Baltimore Wharf now stands, clear round the beach, to the site now occupied by the black-smith Shop of the Quartermaster's Department, and Engineer Boat-house.

The washing of the tide, filling the interstices between the piles forming the foundation of this structure, with sand, caused in time a formation of new ground, compact and solid, upon which the present building now stands.

On the opposite side, on the corner, stands the store of Jas. D. Watkins, built in 1863 ; next we come to the Book Store, William Baulch, Post Trader, proprietor; back of which on the same ground stands the house now occupied by the widow of Gen'l. De Russy. This building has quite a history. Built in 1817, it was at first a Government Stable ; then when the construction of the Fort commenced, large numbers of slaves and military prisoners employed on the works, required a place of confinement and this house was then turned into a prison for their incarceration. About 1842 it was turned into a dwelling-house, since which time it has so remained.

— 28 —

Wending our way slowly along, we see on our right the Office of the Engineering Department, and Fort Monroe Post Office. In the extent of the ground occupied by it, and the other buildings surrounding it, was a Hotel of small dimensions, which during the Rebellion, was turned into a Hospital by General Benj. F. Butler, and afterwards removed by order of the Secretary of War.

St. Mary's Catholic Church, the cornor-stone of which was laid in 1848, Rev. Thomas Murray Pastor, in which Divine Services are held every Sunday morning at 10:30 A. M., and Vespers at 4:30 P. M., in Summer and 7:30 P. M. in Winter, and the only church of any denomination, on the Point, outside the walls of the Fort, next meets the eye of the observer; adjoining which, are two stables, which were used as places of residence for the citizens employed in the Fort. Above these are seen a row of frame buildings erected by the Ordnance Department, about 1838, and used as places of residence. On the right of the road stands a large brick building known as the "Machine Shop," which, during the War, employed between 400 and 500 men ; this building was erected about 1860 and was used for the manufacture of rifled Cannon, axles for heavy sling-carts, and various other utensils of war.

The other buildings on the Point, were principally erected in 1860 and 1861, and were used for the purposes to which they are now devoted, with the exception of the Quarters of the Ordnance Department, adjoining the Machine Shop, and the residence and Office of its Commandant, Major L. S. Babbitt, which are of recent date.

Between the Point and Mill Creek Bridge, lying about a mile distant, were houses, shops, and storehouses, which have since been removed, and the ground devoted to other purposes. On the bridge just referred to is a Picket Guard-house, where the "sentry walks his lonely round," and keeps watch over

Government property and the Reservation, which extends about twenty feet the other side of the Creek.

Traversing the Shell-Road which stretches before us, we see looming in the distance, the town of Hampton, situated three miles from Old Point. As early as 1608, this town was visited by Captain John Smith, and some of his comrades, and they were hospitably entertained by the natives, previous to his starting on his voyage of exploration. It was at that time of very limited dimensions, being a small village, containing only about eighteen houses, and covering an area of three acres of ground. The name by which it was known, then, was Kecoughtan, after a tribe of Indians in the vicinity, who at that time were very small, numbering only about twenty warriors. It was settled by the English as early as 1610, although the name it now bears, was not applied to it, until long afterward. In 1705, the town was incorporated, and received its present name of Hampton.

"In 1794, Hampton is mentioned in the same connection with Norfolk, Richmond, Petersburg, and other towns, thus showing it must have been a place of some importance." This is taken from a work called "Notes on Virginia," by Thomas Jefferson.

Hampton has, at various times, been visited by scourges in the shape of invaders, both in the War of the Revolution, and also in the late War of the Rebelion. "One of the earliest engagements of the Revolutionary War, was the successful defense of the town by the inhabitants, aided by a rifle company, against the boats of a British fleet, in October, 1775. In 1813, the town was less fortunate, being attacked by Admiral Cockburn and Sir Sidney Beckwith, with a flotilla of boats, and captured after a short but decisive action. On this occasion, the place was given up to pillage, and the inhabitants who had been unable to flee, subjected to most shameful indignities and barbarities. Even the British commander, was moved to indignation, at the excesses he was unable to prevent; and answering a congratulation received from his commanding general at Norfolk, deprecated all praises of his achievement, with the forcible and striking remark: "Worthless is the laurel that is steeped in woman's tears."

Again when the war of 1861 broke out, Hampton was destined to still further disaster. The creek upon which the town now stands, was, for awhile, the dividing line between the Union and Confederate forces; the latter occupying the western, the former the eastern side. In August 1861, the Confederate forces, under General Magruder, numbering about seven thousand men, with eight pieces of artillery, were stationed on Back river, about three miles from Hampton. His intention was to force an engagement upon the Union soldiers stationed at Newport News; or at least destroy the town, and thus prevent its being used by General Butler's men as winter quarters. The latter he was successful in doing; as not only every house but one was destroyed, but the long bridge spanning the creek, was burned also."

The preceding paragraph, and the one which immediately follows, we quote from "Visitors' Hand Book of Old Point Comfort. Va., and Vicinity," by C. W. Betts, of the Hampton Normal and Agriculture Institute of Hampton. Va. The succeeding paragraph is the account of the burning of Hampton, by an officer of the Confederate army, who was an eye-witness of, and a participant in, the same. His statement is as follows: "The burning of this beautiful and ancient little town, was not an act of mere wanton and useless destruction; nor was it expected, by those who suggested or carried it into execution, to have any material effect in crippling the operation of the Federal army encamped in its vicinity. But, at that time, the opinion prevailed throughout the North, that the masses of the Southern people, were not in sympathy with the secession movement, but were led, or rather forced along, against their will, and convictions, by defeated and ambitious politicians.   *   *   *   *   *   *

" It became necessary, in some emphatic way, to disabuse the Northern mind, of this entire misconception of the actual condition of affairs, and it was supposed that a scene, such as the burning of a town by its own inhabitants, rather than have it occupied by an invading foe, would tend greatly to the accomplishment of the end.

"This step had several times been suggested to General Magruder, commanding on the Peninsula, and this too, by residents of the town and county ; but he, unwilling to sacrifice the property of citizens who had already suffered so much from the ravages of war, had declined to adopt the suggestion. At length, however, he reluctantly yielded to the wishes of the people.

*   *   *   *   *   *   *   *   *   *

" Having stationed a considerable force at the Whiting Farm, on the New Market road, about five miles from Hampton, he despatched a battalion of four companies from Colonel Hodges regiment, Captain Phillips and Good's companies of cavalry, and Captain Sinclair's company of infantry, to the accomplishment of the enterprise. Captain Phillips's company, Old Dominion Dragoons, was raised in the town and county ; and Captain Sinclair's, the York Rangers, was raised in the county of York, but officered by men from Hampton : the remaining troops were from other portions of Virginia. The whole force was under the command of Colonel Hodges.

*   *   *   *   *   *   *   *   *   *

"Strong guards were sent out on the Newport News and Salter's Creek roads, to prevent a surprise from that direction, as the bridge over the creek which crosses the Back river road, had been burned, and a force obtaining possession of the New Market road, would effectually cut off their line of retreat. A strong picket was also sent out to Hope's farm, on the road leading north from the town.

"The expedition entered Hampton just after nightfall, on the 9th of August, 1861, and immediately proceeded to the work of conflagration. The town as it stood at the time, lay almost entirely on the western bank of Hampton river, and was divided into four nearly equal sections, by King and Queen streets. The plan of operation was simply to assign a detachment to each of these sections with instructions to commence on the eastern side, and fire the houses as they retired.

"Colonel Hodges halted his battalion at a line of breastworks thrown up by the enemy just to the westward of the old church wall, while Captain Phillips took command of the remaining troops, and proceeded to the more active work of the night. After assigning each detachment to its special duty, he himself, proceeded to the foot of Hampton Bridge, to watch any demonstration of the enemy, from the direction of Fort Monroe. After a little brisk firing the Federal pickets retired, and the Confederates were in undisputed possession of the town.

"But few of the houses were occupied; all the arms-bearing population was in the Confederate army; most of the non-combatants had fled to Williamsburg, Richmond and other places when the Federal troops had first occupied Newport News, and the negroes, not carried away by their owners, had, for the most part, sought the protection of the Federal lines. Thus, the town was virtually deserted, only a few old and infirm people, remaining in it. But the most painful part of that night's work, was to inform those few of the dreadful errand on which they had come.

"No time could be given for the removal of effects; what was to be done, had to be done quickly ; so, in fifteen minutes after the citizens had been notified to leave, the work of firing had begun. So finely planned and so admirably executed were the arrangements for this, that in half an hour every house had been fired, and before dawn, the pretty little village was a disfigured heap of smouldering ashes and crumbling walls. Only five houses remained standing, they, from some cause, having failed to burn. Of these five, two were torn down by the Federal troops; and now, there are only two houses on the eastern side of the river, that were built prior to the 7th day of August, 1861.

"It is due to the vindication of General Magruder's character, against the reproaches that have been cast upon it, to say, this act, since so loudly condemned, was, at that time, received with cordial approval. Concurrent testimony amply proves, that, in many cases, property was fired by the hands of its owners, or the children of its owners and this, too, with an alacrity and zeal, altogether unsurpassed."

* * * * * * * * *

From this statement, coming as it does, from an eye-witness of its horrors, it appears that much of the stigma attaching to General Magruder, and his associates, is undeserved, and hearing "both sides of the story," is apt to change the opinion of those, who have always supposed the burning of the beautiful little town, to have been an act on part of the Confederates of wanton cruelty and uncalled-for vandalism.

For some time after the War closed, Hampton was comparatively at a stand-still, and we find nothing worthy of note concerning it. Its population consisting almost entirely of the colored element, were chiefly engaged in the humble occupations of oystering and fishing. Changes in Nations, communities or families, if they are sudden, bring with them a corresponding degree of joy, if agreeable, or, on the other hand, if the change be not an agreeable one, a depression will inevitably ensue, which, for a time, paralyzes all exertion, and utterly prostrates every industry.

This was the state of things financially and commercially, in one of the garden spots of our Country, " the sunny South." Here, where everything had been so flourishing, before the dread Angel of War flapped his dark pinions over her fair territory, bringing destruction and ruin in his train, a sudden stagnation succeeded, and business was utterly at a stand-still. Her wharves, which, ere the tocsin of War with its discordant blast, sounded on the ears of its victims, had been the scene of the liveliest mercantile prosperity, after the advent of this dread monster, presented, to the eye of the observer, a dreary desolation, which could only be conceived by an eye-witness.

Hampton in conjunction with the rest of the South, partook of this general stagnation, and for years, her improvements were insignificant. Gradually, however, she recovered from the shock, and, with the ushering in of the new era, whereby the down-trodden Africans so long oppressed and imposed upon, could enjoy, legally, the same privileges and immunities, as their ever more highly-favored white brethren, a new *regime* was instituted, and improvements, though slow, were sure.

Modern buildings are rapidly supplanting the old houses; manufactures of various kinds, and trade generally, continues to increase; this is largely owing to the fact, that Northern capitalists, with commendable foresight, are beginning to turn their attention to this promising field of investment, and with their advent, and the enterprise accompanying it, a career of prosperity is opening for Hampton, the evidence of which can be seen by any one visiting and viewing the town in its present proportions, and contrasting it with its dimensions as heretofore described.

It is now connected by rail and a line of chariots with Old Point Comfort and by rail with Newport News, of which more will be said in detail hereafter. This innovation, a possibility which the wildest imagination would never have deemed worthy of consideration a moment, a dozen years ago, fully establishes the fact of its advancement and prosperity.

The Chesapeake and Ohio Rail Road have completed a branch of their road, having Chesapeake City, or Mill Creek, as it is familiarly called, for its terminus, the station being named Phœbus Station, after the proprietor of the Hygeia Hotel. Along its route, for a distance of eighty miles or more, points of attraction are continually meeting the eye of the traveler, and by their interest, historically and otherwise, amply repay a visit and investigation. Before entering upon a discussion of their respective merits we will conclude our description of Hampton. To resume: —

The town contains about three thousand inhabitants, principally colored, although, from the facts already narrated, the Caucasian element of its population, is rapidly on the increase, and numbers in its ranks, most of the principal merchants. There are two principal streets, running at right angles with each other, forming the chief thoroughfares. The main one, upon which the bridge opens being named Queen, and its intersecting companion, King. Previous to the War of the Rebellion, Hampton, in comparison with its present proportions, was very limited in extent. The two streets just referred to being the only ones, and, dividing the village, as it then was, into four equal parts, formed a square. The names given to these two streets, was in consistency with a custom, prevalent at the time, of giving to localities, as much as possible, names of English origin ; the observance of this custom is discernible in the names of most of the counties of Virginia, and the English inhabitants of Hampton, with the love of their mother

— 36 —

country still warm in their breasts, exhibited and perpetuated the same, in the names of objects by which they were surrounded in everyday life, and which continually brought to mind their bonny island home.

This same feeling is observable in another class of its inhabitants, viz., the negroes. After the War, when Hampton began to increase in size, and the colored people began to form so large a proportion of its populace, they erected "challies" along what were then merely lanes, bestowing upon these such names as Lincoln, and others of similar character, having in them so much relative to such an important era, in the history of the colored race, and which constantly brought to their minds those patriots, who, by the sacrifice of every comfort and by the yielding up of life itself, succeeded in effecting their emancipation.

The town is rapidly increasing its limits towards Newport News on the west, and the Chesapeake and Ohio Rail Road on the north. It is rapidly comprehending within its boundaries all its suburban surroundings, such as are now known as, "Little England," and "Fox Hill," and will eventually take in Newport News itself.

The chief attraction in this town, so pregnant with historic memories, is Old St. John's Church. It is on the right hand side of Queen Street a short distance above King. In as brief a manner as possible, we will give as much of its history, as we have been able to gather. Under the administration of Sir Thomas Yeardley, in 1621, there was a law passed that a house of worship should be erected, and a burial ground set apart, on every settlement in Virginia. But as Kecoughton was one of the earliest settled places, it is natural to suppose that a church was erected some time previous to this date. The old records place the date at 1620. The new church, (St. John's), was built between 1658 and 1660. The old church was on what is known as the "Pembroke farm," about three-quarters of a mile from St. John's Church on the same road. There are a number of old gravestones still on the place. Among other interments, is that of Sir John Neville, Vice-Admiral of his Majesty's fleet in the West Indies, who died in 1697.

The present Vestry book of the Church dates back no further than 1751, the original having been lost or destroyed. But the records of the Court extend back to 1635, an I furnish interesting and reliable information. The first record we have is that of the church Wardens presenting to the Court an unworthy female in 1644. In the next year we read of a Rev. Mr. Mallory, as performing service and being remunerated for it. In the next year we read of a Rev. Justinian Aylmer, who officiated till 1667. He was succeeded by Jeremiah Taylor who buried a Mr. Nicholas Baker in the *New Church of Kichotan*, according to a request of the deceased in his will. In the same year, Mr. Robert Brough, requests to be buried in the *Old Church of Kichotan*. Thus in the same year there was a new and an old church standing."

Pastors regularly succeeded each other from that time until the present. Prominent among them was the Rev. Mark L. Chevers, who served as Chaplain at Old Point Comfort during the same time, and was known and beloved by all the inhabitants. He served from about 1816 till 1842-43. The present incumbent, Rev. Mr. Gravatt, succeeded his predecessor in 1876.

It is supposed that the bricks used in the construction of the edifice, were brought from England by the early colonists, and although the church has passed through various vicissitudes, yet it has withstood the ravages of time, and the assaults of frenzied foes, and to-day peacefully reposing amid its quiet surroundings, near the "City of the dead," it stands the oldest church in America.

The British forces occupied this edifice during the war of 1812, using it for various purposes, and they destroyed all but the walls. The framework of the bell tower became so decayed about this time, that the "Old Queen Anne" bell, was taken down, and placed in the angle made by the church and tower. However it was removed from that position by order of Major Crutchfield, (who commanded the troops encamped on "Little England Farm") to the guard-house of that encampment, and the tongue becoming loose shortly after, an axe was used to strike the hours, and the bell cracked. It was recast in 1825.

The condition of the church at this time being very dilapidated, it was determined to repair the same, and a meeting was called, vestrymen elected, and means sufficient were raised to defray the expense. Its tribulations, however, were not at an end, as at the beginning of the War of the Rebellion, it was set on fire and burned to the ground by the Confederates ; but the walls were so substantially built, that they withstood even this severe test, and remain a part of the present structure. So intent were its destroyers in their wholesale destruction of this ancient landmark, that excavations were made under each of the four corners, to find the corner-stone, in order to rifle it of whatever treasures it possessed ; whether the vandals were successful or not, history fails to record. There are several ancient graves within its enclosure, the oldest of which is dated 1701. The church is always open to visitors, the key being found at the residence of the sexton but a few doors from the church.

The Post Office, Jail and Court House, are situated on King Street, but a few doors from Queen. The Office of the County Clerk, is in the second story of the Court House, where may be seen the old records, some of which are very interesting, and are shown to visitors, upon application at the clerk's office.

On King Street, a few doors from Barnes's Hotel, stands what may be considered as being second in importance, in the town so far as antiquity goes, it being the only house left of the original town. It is a large brick building, old fashioned in style and substantially built, with high steps in front.

The Baptist and Methodist denominations, have representative churches in the town, both white and colored. The Baptist Church (white) is a remarkably tasty structure on King Street, opposite the Court House. Hampton boasts a very neat bank; it is situated on Queen Street; a brick building; and is one of the ornaments of the town.

Two hotels, Barnes's and the Hotel Comfort, the former on King Street, a few doors from Queen, and the latter on Queen Street, a short distance from the Bridge, and numerous boarding houses, in the town and vicinity, offer their accommodations to the public, and cater to its wants.

Many strange sights meet the eye of the observer, as he traverses the streets of this little southern town. Some of them bring back forcibly reminiscences of the days " befo' de wa'. " In the rear part of the town, removed from its business thoroughfares, resides the element of its population whose mannerisms and peculiarities, preserved to this day as they were in " the palmy days of slavery, " produce the impressions to which we have just referred. Their tumbled down shanties, having nothing in their appearance of either elegance or refinement, but whose uncouth exterior detracts nothing from their value in the eyes of their occupants, are in striking consistency with the manners and characteristics of this proverbially happy people. Knowing but little of the usages of society, and caring less for its fastidious distinctions, the negro smokes his pipe, and plays with his wife and children, with as much gusto, and hilarity, as do his brothers of the white race, in their elegant parlors, and handsomely appointed drawing-rooms. On the steps of these primitive habitations, may be seen their happy occupants, smoking and gossiping over the little events which interest them, after the day's work is done, while the children in Paradisaically scant costume, tumble and roll in merry mirth before the cottage door.

The picture would lack its finishing touch, did it not possess the inevitable canine as its crowning feature, and scarcely a family but possesses its "dorg," whose privileges and liberties, as regards both eating and sleeping, are regarded as sacredly, as are those of any of the rest of the household.

Many styles of equipage, which you would fail to find in the catalogue of any of our fashionable carriage makers, are to be seen in these southern climes. To those accustomed to to look upon nothing but the tasty and elegant "turn-outs," of the fashionable metropolis, these primitive specimens of vehicles have a peculiar interest, and are an attractive feature. Few of them possess any horses, and their only animal of labor, and also for driving, is the steer. It is amusing to see the ingenuity exhibited by some of these humble laborers, in the manufacture of wheeled vehicles. All he seems to need is an axle-tree, and a pair of wheels, and from a few pieces of lumber, and some nails, he will manufacture a useful means of transporting himself, and his articles of merchandise, in which he sits with as lordly a grace, and as much pride, as though it were a coach and four. Sometimes a box is all that is seen above the wheels, and perhaps the animal boasts but one or one and a-half horns, but a "steer's a steer for a'that," and whether pleasuring or doing business he is the negroe's mainstay.

Lying midway between Hampton and Mill Creek, are two points of great interest nationally and locally. We refer to the *National Home for D. V. Soldiers*, and the *Hampton Normal and Agricultural Institute*. The entrance to the *National*

Home, which we will make the first subject of discussion, is a side road, branching off from the main road leading from the Point to Hampton. A large gate-way admits us, which is surmounted by a wooden semicircle: just inside of which is a small guard-house surmounted by a statue of Liberty and used as a rendezvous for the guard while on duty. A pleasant and beautiful gravel carriage-drive, enables the visitors to inspect the grounds from their carriages, and thus gain a general idea of the inclosure, before proceeding to a more minute inspection on foot.

The home is delightfully situated amid its embowering trees and shrubbery, facing Hampton Roads, and at the entrance of Hampton Creek. Previous to the War, it was known as the Chesapeake Female College, under the control of the Baptist denomination. It was built in 1857, at a cost of $64,000, and was occupied about November of the same year, although not entirely finished until the winter of 1859-60. It consisted originally of 40 acres. Here the *elite* of Virginia's aristocracy sent their daughters, and their merry ringing laughter resounded through these halls in the *ante bellum* days, but with the brooding of the dark cloud of war, they were put to a far different use.

In October 1861, it was taken possession of by the Government, and used as a hospital; and afterwards used by General Schofield as Headquarters. It was purchased by General Butler in 1864, who sold it to the Government for its present use in 1870, for which they paid him $50,000.

The Rev. Charles A. Raymond, the former President of the College, was appointed the first Deputy Governor of this Branch, January 1st 1871. During that year the inmates numbered 50, but as the place became better known, and its facilities increased, the number became larger. The number that could be accommodated originally was 350.

On the 17th of January 1873, Captain P. T. Woodfin, the present Governor, was appointed, and under his able management, the capacity of the Home was greatly increased, until its inmates now number between 12,00 or 15,00. New Barracks and Amusement Hall were built, Library enlarged, and the accommodations generally of the home, largely increased. Since its incipiency between 3000 and 4000 inmates, have been relieved and cared for. In 1883, the first quarter, the average number present was 1057; present and absent, over 1200; whole number cared for 1349. The demand from all parts of the country were so frequent, and the applications for admission so numerous, that it became necessary to enlarge the accommodations, and the main building was remodeled; on each of the four floors, the whole front of the building is occupied by broad piazzas, and the strictest attention is paid to the comfort and convenience of the inmates. New buildings are constantly being added, taking the place of the unsightly frame structures, which at the time of its adoption as a home, were hastily constructed to meet the emergencies then existing. The present Officers of the Institution are as follows:— Captain P. T. Woodfin, Governor; Wm. Thompson, Treasurer. Secretary and C. S.; Doctor S. K. Towle, Surgeon. General McClellan is the Local Manager.

There are many attractions in the grounds to visitors. The Main Building, Ward Memorial Hall, Conservatory, Hospital. Library and Reading Room. We will first visit the Main Building. It is approached by a broad flight of steps, which having ascended, we stand on the piazza of the second story. The style of the building, betrays its original use. It has about it still, the air of an Academy, and the architecture of the Building is in consistency with its original use. The entire structure is used for company quarters. It is very neat and clean in all its arrangements, and passing through one might imagine it to be always "inspection day." The inmates are sitting on their bunks, reading, smoking or engaged in any occupation suited to their several tastes, and seem contented and happy.

We pass on to the second, third, fourth and fifth stories, and find them duplicates of the first. From the piazza of the fifth story is obtained a magnificent view of the harbor and Roads. The sight which we can view from this elevated stand-point, more than repays us for the exertion we have expended in reaching it.

Far out at sea, the canvas of an approaching vessel may be seen. It is a picture which must be seen in order to be appreciated. With the canvas "bellied" out with the wind, and the sun rays falling upon it with such a beautiful effect, making her sails seem dazzlingly white, and her keel, hull and masts, forming such a pleasing contrast, she seems instinct with life, and glides upon the surface of the water with a grace and beauty which is almost magical, and to a vivid imagination seems almost spectral.

When approaching from the mouth of the Bay, her different parts loom into view, and her symmetry and beauty become apparent, gradually approaching completeness, it is fitly emblemized by the unvailing of some mighty statue. The cloud canvas rolling back gradually, and disclosing the perfection of the picture concealed beneath.

A more picturesque view than this Harbor, when it is filled with these white-winged sea-birds, can scarcely be conceived. Far as the eye can reach, the tall spire-like masts loom up against the horizon, and seem like the steeples of a great city. At night when each craft hangs out her lights, and twinklingly they glimmer forth into the darkness, the sight, to a spectator at a distance is one long to be remembered ; they seem like the shifting scenes of a panorama, or the populous streets of a great city, teeming with life, and brilliantly lighted with thousands of gas-jets.

Having viewed the Harbor in all its details, we will next ascend to the cupola, from which a bird's-eye view of the entire grounds is obtained. The buildings, and the grounds surrounding them, seen from this altitude, present a very pleasing picture. The floral-arrangements particularly, are shown to advantage by the distance, and their beauty is more decided and apparent than when we are looking at them, when on a level with them. Not only can our immediate surroundings be viewed, but the entire country, for miles, as far as the eye can reach, lays spread out, like a grand canvas painting, before us.

The next building to which the gaze and attention of the observer is drawn is Ward Memorial Hall. The Hall was built from funds bequeathed by Horatio Ward of London. England. The original amount left was $100,000, which with its accumulated interest amounted to $111,000. The amount was divided among different Branches. The following extract is taken from the Minutes of the Board of Managers, and may prove interesting:—

"The President laid before the Board a communication from Messers Farmer and Robbins, of London, solicitors of the late Horatio Ward, announcing that the high Court of Chancery of England, had made a decree ordering the delivery of the Bonds named in the Will of said Horatio Ward, being 15 bonds State of Missouri, $15,000; 25 North Carolina, $25,000: 20 Viriginia, $20,000; 40 Tennesee, $40,000. Total, $100,000; with accumulated interest amounting to $9,700, in United States Bonds; and £250, 9s.6d. cash; to the National Asylum.

"Whereupon the following resolution was adopted:

"*Resolved*, That the Board of Managers of the National

Asylum for Disabled Volunteer Soldiers, being found entitled, under a degree of the high Court of Chancery of England, dated June 4th, 1870, in the suit of Ward *vs* McKervan, to the legacy given by the will of the late Horatio Ward to the National Soldiers' and Sailors' Home in Washington, hereby accept the same in full discharge of the executors of said will, to wit: Benjamin Moran Esq. and Henry Powel Esq.; that ———— be duly authorized and empowered, as the certain attorney of the Board of Managers, to receive the Bonds with the accrued interest, as invested, and also any cash balance there may be; and due acquittance and discharge for the same to make to the said executors; and that the power of attorney accompanied with this resolution, under the seal of the Asylum, and certified by the President and Secretary, be also signed by the President of the United States, and Secretary of War, as ex-officio members of the Board.

Resolved: — In grateful acknowledgment of the magnificent donation to the National Asylum for Disabled Volunteer Soldiers, by the late Horatio Ward of London, England,——that a suitable Tablet be inscribed as follows: " The Ward Home for Disabled Soldiers," and placed upon the principal building of the Southern Branch."

The above shows the appropriateness of the title bestowed upon the building, and is also a testimonial to the charity and benevolence of the donator. In this building is the large, airy, dining room, containing sixteen long tables capable of seating 1,000 men; on the same floor is the kitchen containing all the appurtenances of a first-class hotel kitchen. The bread is supplied from a Bakery on the grounds, and is of the best quality. The bill of fare changes daily, and embraces good substantial food, such as is calculated to preserve good health and afford them what is pleasant and palatable.

The Bill of Fare below will give an idea of what they generally consist. While it contains few of the luxuries, yet all its items are healthful and nutritious: —

Breakfast	Dinner	Supper
Ham	Roast Beef	Stewed Prunes
Bread	Bread	Bread
Potatoes	Butter	Butter
Eggs	Potatoes	Cheese
Butter	Rice Pudding	Tea
Coffee	Coffee	

There is also a fine Billiard Hall and Theatre in the second story of the Hall. The Billiard Hall is large and furnished with first class tables at which the inmates can amuse themselves at pleasure. The Theatre is as fine a little Opera House, as can be found within the limits of any city, and affords a means for the gratification of the lovers of the "Drama," whose tastes are sometimes catered to by travelling Troupes of first class ability, and sometimes by the "Home Troupes," of which there are two connected with the same, Theatrical and Minstrel. The Offices of the Commandant, Secretary, Sergeant Major, and Treasurer, are in a neat brick building called "Headquarters," situated to the right of Ward Hall. The Conservatory, containing a fine collection of rare exotics, well repays a visit, and here can be purchased flowers made into any desirable shape.

The Hospital with its world of untold suffering, and manifold examples of heroism next attracts our attention. Here may be seen those who for country's sake and Liberty have sacrificed so much of their lives and happiness. What groundwork for tales of fiction of enchancing interest, could the novelist find in many of these unwritten lives, full of romance and doomed to suffering and death, as the reward of their devotion.

On the second floor of the first building on the left, as we enter the grounds, are the Library, Reading and Smoking Rooms. The Library has been supported principally by contributions, the first of which was made by the "Ladies Union" of New York in 1871. Since then donations have been made by many parties whose memories of the deeds of valor performed by these heroes, induced them to show, by this means, a slight appreciation of their merits. Among them may be mentioned, Mrs. General McClellan, Mrs. Zollikoffer and Mr. Albert Crane of New York City, Mrs. Oswin Wells, Mrs. J. Watson Black, Mrs. Whitmore, Mrs. J. H. Goodwin, Miss Batterson, and Mr. Black, of Hartford, Conn., and many others.

Governor Woodfin, always anxious to secure every comfort and enjoyment to the inmates, has taken a great interest in the Library, and has made many choice and interesting additions to the same, till they now number over four thousand volumes. The works comprise editions in three different languages — American, German and French. There are one hundred and forty-six papers taken, twenty-six of them being daily, five tri-weekly, and one hundred and fifteen weekly ; besides magazines and other periodicals. The Library is open daily from 8 A. M. to 12 M., and from 1 to 5 P. M.; also from 6 to 8 P. M. It is closed on Saturday afternoon from 1 to 6 o'clock.

Besides the points of interest already described a great many other attractions present themselves to the visitor, and claim his attention. A magnificent drive skirts the water's edge, from which a beautiful view of the Roads and Bay, can be seen. A beautiful promenade, consisting of a broad board terrace, runs the whole length of the breakwater, and is used by the inmates as a promenade, and conduces both to their health and comfort.

Great care has been taken, and a lavish expenditure has been made, in tastefully laying out, and beautifully shading the grounds, and a more admirably arranged, or more suitably situated object for the purpose for which it was intended, could not be imagined.

A well organized Fire Department, whose efficacy has been thoroughly tested, especially in Hampton, at the late fire, April 10th, 1884, where its efficiency and skill were most clearly exhibited, adds its quota to the numerous and valuable auxiliaries of this Institution, and prove it to be not merely an ornamenal appendage.

On the grounds a well fitted up, and fully equipped "Sutler Store," furnish the inmates with articles of comfort and necessity.

The entertainments in "Ward Memorial Hall," theatrical and otherwise, enliven the tedium of an otherwise humdrum existence, but are by no means the only sources of amusement, as boating, yatching, fishing and salt-water bathing (the houses for this purpose being erected on the dock at the mouth of the creek), combine to render the life of the inmates pleasant and happy.

Open Air Concerts, by the Military Band connected with the Institution, from 2 to 4 P. M., daily, (Sundays excepted) are another pleasing feature of each day's doings in this magnificent evidence of a nation's gratitude to her veterans.

Every Sunday Morning at 9:30 A. M., an *Outside Inspection* occurs. In this ceremony about 1,000 of the veterans participate, and in their uniforms, grouped about the spacious walks in companies, afford a picturesque and interesting view to a spectator.

A great many souvenirs, both fanciful and curious, can be secured by visitors, from the inmates, many of whom employ their spare time in this artistic and pleasing occupation. A farm of 150 acres, about three miles distant from the Home, from which valuable produce for the consumption of the inmates is obtained, adds to the value of the Home property.

Taking our leave of the Home grounds, we will next visit the National Cemetery, where, reposing amid its weeping willows, and quiet surroundings, sleep our martyred dead. — Here sleep those Sons of Freedom, whose blood cemented the foundations of the Nation's superstructure, and achieved those glorious victories, whose consequences and results will be felt as long as our Republic has an existence.

It is situated on the south-eastern side of the grounds of the Normal School, and is separated from the Soldiers' Home, by a narrow inlet of the Hampton Creek. It consists of an irregular lot, many-sided, six of which are right lines, and the remainder following the windings of the inlet above mentioned. A desultory glance would convey the idea, that it formed a parallelogram, twice as long as it was wide, but a more careful examination, would prove its fallacy. It contains 11.61 acres of level land, and was purchased by the United States in 1867 for the sum of $6,306.

It is enclosed by a rubble stone wall, laid in mortar, and covered by a rough coping.

Entering on the North side by a gate, we proceed to the Superintendent's Office, and register our names; after which we proceed on our tour of inspection. Flower beds garnish the sides of the main avenue, which is a broad pathway 20 feet wide. The flag-staff surmounts a mound 350 feet from the entrance. Large cannon planted vertically flank the mound on each side. Here paths diverge to both right and left of the main walk.

A large solid granite monument rises in imposing proportion, near the centre of the grounds, and attracts the eye of the observer long before he reaches the enclosure of the Cemetery. An iron fence, composed of 3 inch rifled cannon

(Rodman), and the pickets, musket barrels with bayonets fixed, enclosing a circular grass plat 74 feet in diameter, forms, an appropriate surrounding for this colossal memento, erected to the memory of the Union troops, who fell to defend their beloved country from disunion and ruin.

This monument is 63 feet in height, and was erected through the exertions of Miss D. L. Dix of New York.

Entering a cemetery, one naturally looks for mounds surmounting the different graves, betokening the presence of the quiet sleepers beneath, but we fail to perceive them ; and were we not aware of its character, and were it not for the presence of the low tombstones, which stand at the head of each grave, we would imagine, and reasonably too, that we were entering some well kept park ; the ground is perfectly level, and the grass is kept closely cropped and the cemetery appears carpeted with a beautiful green.

A marked distinction is observable in the southern portion of the grounds, the headstones here being all composed of wood, while the rest are stone. A reason for this will instantly suggest itself to the spectator, and it is easily assigned. The occupants of these graves were Confederates, who died while prisoners of war, either at the hospital at Camp Hamilton, or Fort Monroe.

That such a marked distinction should exist is to be extremely deprecated, as it seems to betoken a spirit of revenge, and unbecoming animosity, which, while it may not be intentional, reflects but little credit upon so great and glorious a Nation as our own. If for no other reason than a refutation of this apparent spleen, the matter should be looked into, and head stones supplied in place of the unsightly wooden ones.

The interments from the Home average five a month. Nearly 6000 interments had been made up to May 1st 1883. The bodies were brought, in many cases, from the places of original interment in the grounds of the general hospitals in the vicinity: many from Big Bethel, Newport News, Norfolk, Craney Island, Portsmouth, and other places.

It is a melancholy reminder of the terrible effects of War, when red-handed and vengeance-breathing it stalks through the land, marring its fair beauty, and carrying death and destruction in its wake.

On coming out, we see a long frame building with a small steeple in front. This is *Bethesda Chapel*, built during the war, by the Presbyterian Missionary Society of New York, in which religious services are held every Sabbath morning at 10:45 A. M., by the Normal School. It has been twice ordered to be removed, but, through the interposition of the officers and friends of the School, the order has been countermanded each time.

The building has a great many historic interests connected with it, which make it of more than ordinary moment to the visitor. One, in particular, we cite. Our martyred and well beloved Garfield, delivered his last public address to the Students of the Normal School in it, on June 5th 1881, about one month previous to his assassination. Below is the address, given impromptu, and bearing the stamp of philanthropy and large heartedness: —

"As I drove through these grounds to-day, I was impressed with the thought that I was between the representatives of the past and the future. Crippled and bent with service and years, those veterans, in the Soldiers' Home, represent the past. You represent the future — the future of your race — a future made possible by the past, by these graves around us.

Two phases of the future strikes me as I look over the assemblage. For I see another race here; a race from the far West. These two classes of the people are approaching the great problem of humanity, which is *Labor*, from different sides.

I put that problem into four words : *Labor must be free.* And for those of you from the far West I would omit the last word, in order to enforce the lesson. To you I would say: *Labor must be!* — for you, for all. Without it there can be no civilization. The white race has learned that truth. They came here as pioneers, felled the forests, and swept away all obstacles before them, by labor. Therefore to you I would say that without labor you can do nothing. The first text in your civilization is ; Labor must be !

You of the African race have learned this text, but you learned it under the lash. Slavery taught you that labor must be. The mighty voice of war spoke out to you, and to us all, that labor must be forever *free*. The basis of all civilization is that Labor must be. The basis of everything great in civilization, the glory of our civilization, is, that Labor must be free.

I am glad that General Armstrong is working out this problem on both sides -- reaching one hand to the South, and one hand to the West — with all the continent of Anglo-Saxon civilization behind him ; working it out in the only way it can be worked out — the way that will give us a country without sections, a people without stain."

The Hampton Normal and Agricultural Institute, next engages our attention. Situated about two and a-half miles from Old Point Comfort, on an estate of one hundred and twenty acres, on what was once known as "Little Scotland," it was during the Civil War, known as "Camp Hamilton," the base Hospital of the Army of the James. As many as 15,000 sick and wounded Union soldiers, were gathered here, and cared for, at one time.

The estate was purchased in the summer of 1867 for $19,000. Through its trustee, Hon. Josiah King, $10,000 of this amount was paid by the "Avery" fund, and the remainder, by the Missionary Association of New York. The necessary buildings were erected, and the school was formally opened, in April, 1868, with fifteen scholars and two teachers. In June 1870, the Institution was chartered by the General Assembly of Virginia. This Charter created a corporation, having power to choose its own successors, and exempting its property from taxation. The Board consists of seventeen members, who hold and control the entire property of the School, by deed from the American Missionary Association.

In March 1872, the General Assembly granted the Institution one-third of the Agricultural College land grant of Virginia. This share, comprising one hundred thousand acres, was sold two months afterward for $95,000. Nine-tenths of this sum was invested in State bonds paying an annual interest of 6 per cent. The other tenth was used in the purchase of additional land, swelling the size of the home farm to one hundred and ninety acres. The annual interest is paid by the State, and supplies one-fifth of the running expenses of the School.

The expenditures must be ratified by a Board of six curators (three of whom may be colored) appointed by the Governor every four years. Besides the property immediately attached to the Home, about four miles from Hampton there is a grain farm of six hundred acres, worked by students, and called the "Hemenway" farm. The entire property of the Institution valued at some $400.000, with the exception of about $45.000, has been paid for by private subscription. Each contributor receives an annual report of the receipts and expenditures, salaries, as well as the gain or loss of each branch of industry.

The prime object of the Institution, is to furnish the Negro race with a corps of competent, energetic, practical teachers : but the demand greatly exceeds the supply, and is increasing yearly.

In April, 1878, Indian students were first admitted, the first arrival of which, consisted of seventeen Arapahoe, Cheyenne and Kiowa warriors, taken from a band of fifty, who had been held as prisoners of war at St. Augustine, Florida, for three years, under Capt. R. H. Pratt, of the U. S. Army. The good accomplished with these, the most savage of the Indian race, led to still further efforts on their behalf, and now the number of Indian students is 108, representing both sexes- fifteen agencies, and as many different tribes. The students for the year ending June 30th, 1883 were as follows : —

Negro Students	Male 277	
" "	Female 198	—475
Indian Students	Male 66	
" "	Female 41	—107
Total		582

This shows the vast amount of good which is being accom. plished, and which may well fill the hearts of those engaged in the enterprise, with pride and gratitude.

Of the 50 officers and teachers in class room, agricultural workshop, and housekeeping departments, 13 are graduates of the School. Ninety per cent. of the four hundred and fifty-two graduates are teaching, or have taught in this and neighboring states.

Classes may be visited each week-day, except Monday, between 10:30 and 12 o'clock A. M.

The *work shops* may be visited any week-day, morning or afternoon.

The *dinner hour* is 12:20 P. M., at which time all the students assemble in the large dining room in Virginia Hall. On *Saturday's only*, the School Band plays during this hour. *Battalion Drill* on Saturdays, from 4 to 5 P. M. *Inspection* every morning, except Sunday and Monday, at 8:15. *Church Ser-*

vices in the chapel in the National Cemetery, on Sunday mornings, at 10:45 o'clock. Seats free.

Starting on our tour of inspection, after visiting the Offices of the Principal and Treasurer, situated in a plain and substantial brick building facing Hampton Creek, we will first visit the LIBRARY and READING ROOM, on the upper floor of this building. Many curiosities of both African and Indian origin are here arranged in groups in show-cases; together with 2600 volumes, and many of the leading newspapers and periodicals of the day. The POST OFFICE is also in this building.

We will next proceed to ACADEMIC HALL, situated between the Office building and the Saw Mill. It is divided into class-rooms, while on the upper floor is a large room for prayer meetings and other purposes. The HUNTINGTON INDUSTRIAL WORKS, the munificent gift of C. P. Huntington, Esq., President of the Chesapeake and Ohio Rail Road Company, next engages our attention. Here are manufactured window-sash, door-frames, scroll work, and mouldings. Both white and colored mechanics are employed here. The lower floor is used for the manufacture and dressing of plain lumber; the second floor for circular sawing, scroll sawing, turning. &c., while the third floor is used as a store and drying room. Mr. Albert Howe is business manager of this department.

The new MACHINE SHOP, in charge of Mr. J. B. H. Goff, is the next point of attraction. All the gas and steam fitting, also the repairing of machinery, is done here. Leaving this building we pass, on our way, two frame cottages called "Marquand" and "Graves" cottage respectively. They contain boys' domitories.

The next place which engages our attention, is THE "STONE" MEMORIAL BUILDING, which was erected by the liberal contribution of Mrs. Valeria Stone of Malden, Mass., who gave $20,000 toward its erection. We come first to the GIRLS INDUSTRIAL ROOM and SEWING and TAILORING DEPARTMENT. Here all the mending and making of garments are done, and uniforms for the sudents are made. Here also we can purchase souvenirs of our visit to this Institution — articles made by Indian and colored students — such as decorated pottery, paper knives, dressed dolls, needle handiwork, &c. Miss M. T. Galpin has general charge, and Mr. R. H. Hamilton is in charge of the Tailoring Department. On the same floor is the KNITTING DEPARTMENT, where the manufacture of mittens is carried on.

We next visit the PRINTING OFFICE and BOOK BINDERY on the first floor also. Two large cylinder and two job presses run by steam, despatch mechanical printed matter of every description. From twelve to fifteen hands are at work, bo h colored and Indian. This department publishes two periodicals, the *Southern Workman* and the *African Repository* a quarterly magazine of the American Colonization Society. Samples of each will be furnished upon application. The Office is in charge of C. W. Betts Esq. The upper floors are used for dormitories.

The next building is the CONSERVATORY, built in 1883. Here can be obtained cut flowers in any shape desired. The WIGWAM built in 1876 and containing dormitories for the Indian boys, and the BARN built in 1878, next attract our attention. Here can be seen specimens of the finest breed of cattle, swine an poultry. In rear of the Barn, on the corner facing the Main Road to Hampton and Old Point Comfort, is the INDIAN TRAINING SHOP, containing CARPENTER SHOP on the first floor, HARNESS and TIN SHOPS; on the second floor the SHOE

DEPARTMENT. There is also a PAINT SHOP connected with the establishment. In an adjoining building is the WHEELWRIGHT and BLACKSMITH SHOPS.

The GYMNASIUM and LAUNDRY between the Training Shop and Boiler House, are the next objects of interest. We have now exhausted all the points of interest, save two. "WINONA" LODGE and VIRGINIA HALL, the latter, the largest and handsomest building on the grounds. The former we will visit first. It was built in 1882, and is intended for Indian girls only. We next enter VIRGINIA HALL by an enclosed walk, and taking our position on the front porch we witness the procession of the students marching to dinner, led by the School Brass Band composed of 16 pieces. This is only on Saturdays. They file into the large dining room, and at the tap of the bell all is profound silence.

At a signal, the entire school join in a vocal thanksgiving for the food, the impressiveness of which must be witnessed, in order to be appreciated. At the tap of the bell, the students are all seated, and do ample justice to the healthful and nutritious food, placed in abundance before them.

The building is 190 feet front by 40 feet in width, with a wing of 100 feet running to the rear. The Bakery and Commissary Department are in the basement. The teachers' and students' dining rooms are on the first floor. The second and third floors contain the rooms of the teachers an l colored students. On this floor are also the teachers, and scholars' parlors. A large and well lighted chapel, with a sitting capacity of 800, is on the third floor. The funds for the erection of this building were the proceeds of a three years' singing tour of the "Hampton Students," and was erected in 1874.

The BOILER and GAS HOUSE are immediately in the rear of Virginia Hall, and supplies the heat for it and Wiona Lodge ;

it also supplies gas for all the principal buildings on the place. It has a capacity of 5000 lights. The bricks used in the erection of these buildings were mostly made by the students on the school grounds.

The last building which engages our attention, is at the entrance of the grounds, and is named the "BUTLER" SCHOOL HOUSE, which was erected by the Government during the war as a school for contrabands, and named after General Butler, who was then in charge of affairs. It is now used as a day school, maintained by the county for six months in the year, and the Normal School for three months, which supplies the teachers. The best time for visiting this school is about 12:30 P. M. There are kitchen and garden drills, and singing from 12:30 to 1:30 P. M., on Mondays and Wednesdays.

The head of the institution, through whose able management it has prospered, to whose unwavering zeal much of its success is due, and whose tireless energy has placed it upon a foundation challenging the admiration and gratitude of all interested in these wards of the Nation, is the Principal, General S. C. Armstrong, whose efforts are ably seconded by the Treasurer, General J. F. B. Marshall, and whose care of the financial interests of the concern, adds no small quota to its prosperity. The Business Manager, Mr. C. F. Briggs, superintends generally the various departments, under whom are able and competent assistants.

Just at the turn of the road, we see, on our left, the old Tyler mansion, the former residence of our ex-President; next we come to the Bridge spanning Hampton Creek. It has been moved a little beyond the site occupied by the old bridge existing in the days of General Magruder, but some of the old posts are still standing, and can be seen at low tide. Crossing the Bridge we are in the town of Hampton, a sketch of which has already been given.

The extension of the Chesapeake and Ohio Railway, from Richmond, through the counties of Henrico, Charles City, New Kent, James City, York, Warwick and Elizabeth City, to Newport News and thence to Phoebus Station, Old Point, opens an interesting and historical country to the visitors at our summer resort, the Hygeia Hotel, whose enterprising head, H. Phoebus, Esq., furnishes communication by Ombus with Phoebus Station, and thus opens this repository of interest and beauty to all his patrons.

Entering the train of which there are two daily, a ride of from twenty-five minutes to half an hour brings us to Newport News, whose mercantile and commercial advantages are recognizable at a glance. A short historical sketch of it may not come amiss. About the beginning of the seventeenth century, Captain Newport landed on the northeastern shore of the James River, bringing supplies and fresh colonists, to the feeble remnant of the first colony planted there. The spot where he landed is about nine miles from Fortress Monroe, and has ever since been known by the odd name of Newports News, or, as it is now commonly abbreviated, Newport News.

There is no where in the world a place that seems better fitted to be the center of an extensive commerce; where the largest ships in the world could float at wharves of ordinary length. The point has a rounded outline, with a beautiful beach, over which the water ripples without a stain. Only a dozen yards from the shore the natural depth is sufficient for vessels of 1000 tons burden, and increases rapidly in advancing toward mid-channel. On the left lie Hampton Roads, Newport News being its upper limit. In that part of Hampton Roads, just below Newport News, occurred the famous battle between the Merrimac and Monitor, a description of which is given in our first chapter.

The shore of Newport News rises abruptly from the beach. in a small bluff about twenty-five feet high, beyond which lies a broad and level plateau; the elevation of which increases toward the east, until it attains an altitude of about forty feet. The inclination from the rear of the proposed city to the shore, will be very gentle, and drainage perfect.

It has never been a place of much importance, and its advantages, commercially and otherwise, have been but lately discovered and recognized. The land upon which the city stands, is owned by the Old Dominion Land Company, and about one thousand acres have been regularly laid out in streets and avenues, the majority of which are graded. Many have been the improvements in the last four years. Handsome residences and stores, both brick and frame, have been erected, wharves where ships of the largest tonnage land and discharge their cargoes, a gigantic grain elevator, and numerous other improvements, give an air of mercantile importance and commercial prosperity, to a neighborhood, which, previous to the time mentioned, consisted of nothing but vacant lots.

The importance and value of its magnificent water front was recognized by those who were pioneers in the opening up of this embryo metropolis, and was evidenced by the fact that before a house or store was erected, an immense covered wharf 700 feet 6 inches long, and 132 feet wide, was built. "A large coal pier — 800 feet long and 50 feet wide — has also been erected. This has two tracks in the centre, and one raised on each side ; being constructed to move the cars by gravity. It is 30 feet high, and vessels are loaded by the twelve chutes from the cars. In the rear of this pier is a mamoth coal pocket, 12,009 feet in length, 70 feet wide, and 35 feet high."

"There is also another covered wharf used by the Old Dominion Steamship Company. This is 800 feet long and 162 feet wide, and is used as a passenger pier. It is two stories high, and connected with a six-story grain elevator 385 x 90 feet, which has a capacity of 1,500,000 bushels."

Vessels of the largest tonnage can approach these wharves at any time, there being 28 feet of water at low tide. English, American, Brazilian, and in fact almost every description of merchantmen, land at the wharves and discharge their cargoes. A line of Brazilian steamers lands here. A park, which has been partially completed, is an attractive feature, and adds to beauty of the city.

The unequalled natural advantages need not be dwelt upon; the harbor on which it is situated, being the finest in the world, and the only one in the United States which can be safely entered without a pilot. There is no bar at the entrance of Chesapeake Bay, and a dozen navies could ride there abreast. The News is but fifteen miles from the open sea, while New York is twenty, Boston about fifty, Philadelphia about one hundred, and Baltimore one hundred and sixty. These considerations afford a basis for judgment, and prove conclusively, this spot in our country destined to have a glorious history in the future of our nation.

Continuing our railway journey, about 17 miles from Newport News, we reach Lee Hall in York County, five miles to the left of which is Yorktown, famous both as being the scene of the surrender of Cornwallis, and also the centennial in 1881. A memorial column, commemorative of the great event, recently ordered by Congress, is in process of erection.

Nine miles further on we come to Williamsburg, containing many interesting relics of Revolutionary times, as well as historic reminiscences of the early history of the colonies.

This place, called "Middle Plantations," when first settled by colonists from Jamestown, in 1632, is now a quaint, unique town; of 1200 or 1500 inhabitants — quiet, dreamy and bearing about its very atmosphere an air of repose, pregnant, however, with historic interest. Suggestions of "days that were," meet us on every side, and seem to render even its dwellings and thoroughfares, ancient and antiquated. Relics of the pomp and glory of King and Crown, long since departed, still exist even in the names of streets, and such names as, "Duke of Gloucester," "Queen," "Henry," and "Palace," seem to carry us back to the days, when good Queen Bess, George IV, and their compeers,reigned in regal splendor, and exercised their sway over our fair territory.

In 1698, the seat of government was removed here by George Nicholson, after the Jail and Statehouse at Jamestown, had been destroyed by fire; Williamsburg, being "healthier, more convenient, and free from moscheloes." Here the royal functionary held his mimic court, small but brilliant, and gay with the court costumes of the period — especially during the sessions of the House of Burgesses, when the streets were alive with chariots and coaches of the nobility and gentry, with cavaliers magnificently mounted, and when every house displayed a profuse and costly hospitality.

Interesting and historic remnants still remain. On Gloucester street, is the site of the old Capitol, burnt in 1746, rebuilt and again burnt in 1832. A few years later, a female college was erected on the same spot, and that too, was destroyed during the late war. Diagonally across the street may still be seen the old Chancery-Office, now a private residence, remodelled, but containing the English bricks and timbers which composed the original structure. *Raleigh Tavern*, the scene of many a midnight revel, and containing committee rooms of patriots, who within their walls discussed the interests of the feeble colonists, is now used as a store-house. Here Richard Henry Lee originated the plan of corresponding committees among the colonies. Higher up the street is the identical magazine from which, in 1775, Lord Dunmore removed the powder belonging to the colony, and stored it on the Magdalen sloop-of-war, an act which roused the indignation of the country, almost as much as the first shot at Fort Sumter, in 1861. It is now used as a stable, and the boys call it THE OLD POWDER HORN. The Colonial Court House, the site of Dunmore's palace, the old Masonic Hall, Tazewell Hall, and especially the ivied church, built in 1680, of imported bricks, with its mural tablets, and its church-yard filled with antique tombstones with their queer inscriptions, will afford a fund of interest for the traveler, and give him food for abundant mental reflection. Here also is the seat of William and Mary College, chartered February 19th, 1693, three times burned, (in 1705, 1859, and 1862,) and it awakens a deeper interest, and excites more curiosity, than all the other buildings combined. From this institution, four signers of the Declaration of Independence, three Presidents of the United States, one Chief-Justice, two United States Attorney-Generals, twenty members of the United States House of Representatives, fifteen United States Senators, seventeen Governors of Virginia and other states, thirty-seven judges of the United States and Virginia, and Lieutenant General Winfield Scott of the United States Army, received their degrees. The present structure contains the original walls, so often tested by fire. The Eastern Lunatic Asylum, in Williamsburg, is the oldest institution of its kind in America, having been founded in 1773.

The battle of Williamsburg, was fought May 5th, 1862, between McClellan's advance and Johnston's rear guard, under Longstreet, and was claimed as a victory by both sides, serving as a temporary check in the advance on Richmond. Between Oriana and Newport News, two miles to the left of the road, is Big Bethel, the scene of the first important battle after the fall of Sumter in 1861.

In the neighborhood of Williamsburg is the site of Jamestown, a spot of more than ordinary interest, the only relic of which is a ruined church tower. Unless measures are taken to preserve it, this too will soon disappear, and naught but water, cover a tract of country, brimming full of historic recollections, having been the scene of so much endurance and so many victories in the history of our forefa s.

Two engagements occurred near Jamestown just before the battle of Yorktown — the first, on June 25th, 1781, between Lieut. Col. Butler, of the Pennsylvania line, and Lieut. Col. Simcoe, of the British army, resulting in a drawn battle, the former supposing that he was only attacking the rear-guard of the enemy, when, in fact, he was engaging the main body of Cornwallis' army. Night saved LaFayette from destruction.

Beyond the Chickahominy lies the county of New Kent, also historic ground. At the residence of a Mr. Chamberlayne, in this county. Washington met the Widow Curtis, whom he aftewards married at the White-House, on the Panumkey river, where McClellan had his base of supplies in 1862. On Wall Creek, in New Kent, is the Mysterious Stone House, of doubtful origin, but supposed to have been built by Capt. John Smith as a fort. It is perhaps, the most curious historic relic in Virginia, an enigma at best.

We next enter Charles City County, one of the original shires into which Virginia was divided, in 1634. Though shorn of its original proportions, it is redolent of Colonial and Revolutionary history, and enjoys the reputation of being the birthplace of two presidents of the United States—viz., Wm. Henry Harrison and John Tyler. The fathers of these presidents were as illustrious as their sons. Benjamin Harrison, a member of the Continental Congress, would have been president of that body after the death of his brother-in-law, Peyton Randolph, had he not yielded in favor of John Hancock, and declined to allow his name to be put in nomination. It was Benjamin Harrison, who, in July of that year, reported the Declaration of Independence framed by Thomas Jefferson. In 1772 he became Governor of Virginia, and was accounted one of the best the State ever had. John Tyler, Sr., (father of the President), a leading patriot of the Revolution, was elected Governor in 1808, and afterwards was United States District Judge. President Tyler was born on James river five miles below Berkely, the birthplace of President Harrison.

Passing from Charles City county, and crossing the Chickahominy at the Long Bridge, now Roxbury Station, we enter Henrico County. This station is not far from *the spot where Capt. John Smith was captured by the Indians.* Many points of interest during the memorable campaign of 1864 — viz., Bethesda Church, Second Cold Harbor, Fort Harrison, and the Dutch Gap Canal, are within easy horseback rides of stations along the line of the Chesapeake and Ohio Rail Road.

Within easy distance of the railway, are the scenes of the famous *Seven Day's Battles Around Richmond*, beginning with Mechanicsville, June 26th, 1862 ; Gaines's Mill and Cold Harbor June 27th ; Savage Station June 29th ; Frazier's Farm, June 30th, and ending at Malvern Hill, July 1st, 1862. The details of these battles, long since familiar to every American school boy, render their names topics of interest, and throw around them a halo of historic importance which must ever make them objects of research, and points of never failing attraction to the traveler. McClellan was driven to the shelter of his gunboats at Harrison's Landing, on the James, and the capitol of the Confederacy was temporarily saved.

It is related that at Frazier's Farm, or Glendale, as it is some times called, Stonewall Jackson, exhausted with loss of sleep, for the first and only time failed to respond to Gen. Lee's order, and did not cross the Chickahominy, thus enabling McClellan to rally at Malvern Hill, which lies two miles to the right of the road. The Confederates here met with a severe repulse. From Harrison's Landing, or Westover, McClellan embarked to join Pope in Northern Virginia.

About seven miles from Richmond, at Fort Lee Station, is the battle-field of Fair Oaks or Seven Pines, fought May 31st, 1862, in which Gen. Joseph E. Johnston was wounded, an accident which brought Gen. R. E. Lee to the front, and gave the army of Northern Virginia its renowned commander. Continuing our journey, on the right of Church-Hill Tunnel, lies Powhatan, the residence in former years of the Mayo family — a spot named for the Indian Chief, the father of Pocahontas, who here held his court. Here too, it is said, the rescue of Smith took place, and the story whether mythical or otherwise, is dear to the hearts of all Virginians. A few miles further, and we dash into the city of Richmond, the Keystone of the Rebellion, and holding within its limits a wealth of historic recollections, which to the antiquarian, affords a fund of useful and entertaining information.

Having thus given our traveler an insight into the surroundings of Fort Monroe, we will make a retrograde movement, and come back to Old Point which having discussed in its geographical and geological outlines, we will enter the Fort itself.

Old Point Comfort, is situated at the extremity of a level, sandy beach, from the southern end of the western shore of the Chesapeake Bay. Its geographical position is. $37°2'$ North Latitude, and $76°12'$ West Longitude, from the meridian of Greenwich. The peninsula is almost entirely surrounded by water. The exception to this, is a strip of beach, some 400 yards wide, which runs to the north and looks eastward.

Over this strip of beach, during heavy easterly storms, with a full spring tide, the sea washes, rendering at such times, the peninsula, an island. On the east, northeast, and southeast, are the waters of the Chesapeake Bay. On the south and southwest, are those of Mill Creek, which empties into, and is fed from, the Hampton Roads. The connections of the peninsula with the main land, are by the narrow strip of land above referred to, and by a bridge over Mill Creek, approached by an artificial causeway, some half mile in length.

The fort is built at the extremity of the peninsula and commands the entrance to Hampton Roads, into which empties the water of the James, Elizabeth and Nansemond rivers. The waters on all sides of the fort are salt, augmented or diminished in intensity by the fresh water floods coming down the James river; though at all times, and in all tides, they are highly saline. The country between the point of the peninsula and York river, distant twenty miles north, and thence across to the James, is cut up by numerous small streams, which are more or less brackish, as the rains are profuse or scanty.

These small streams all communicate with the Chesapeake, Hampton Roads, or the James. The land upon which the fort is built is some four feet above mean high-water mark. Salt marshes are on the northeast of the fort, but these seem to have but little, if any effect, upon its sanitary condition.

The geological formation of the peninsula upon which the fort is built, is ocean sand resting upon marl impregnated clay. Boring to the depth of 800 feet, within the inclosure of the fort, has shown nothing but sand, lying upon marl impregnated clay, with here and there small veins of sharp bluish sand ot fine grain, admirably adapted for polishing and grinding metals. The country on the main land is flat, and there are no hills within a radius of eight or ten miles. The soil to the north of Mill Creek, which bounds the reservation in that direction, is aluminous and quite productive, giving, under favorable circumstances, abundant yields of wheat, corn, oats, potatoes, as well as of all the market vegetables. There are few portions of the country more suitable for trucking farms than the vicinity of Fort Monroe, there being no rocks of any description in the neighborhood.

The whole country to the north and northwest of the fort, is underlaid by extensive beds of marl, at depths varying from 20 to 50 feet. The water procurable from wells, on the mainland, is, in consequence, quite unpalatable, and recourse has therefore to be made to cisterns for a supply of drinking water. All, previous to the war of secession, who possessed the means, erected them for the purpose of collecting rain-water. On the Chesapeake Bay beach, distant some 2000 yards to the north, are heavy sand hills, and on and around these are found live oaks as well as the southern pine. This is said to be the most northern position in the United States at which the live oak is to be met with.

In the gardens of the fort are to be found numerous fig trees, which flourish exceedingly well, though the fruit crop of them cannot be relied upon, as the late frosts of spring oftentimes destroy them. The forests and woodlands in the neighborhood, on the mainland, furnish the varieties of forest trees, bushes and shrubs usually met with in the middle region of the United States.

The waters surrounding the fort are well stocked with fish, principally rock, sheephead, bay mackerel, trout, white perch, sun, spot, hog, chub, green flounders, moss-bunkers, and, toad. Porpoises are quite numerous, and white shark not scarce. Crabs, both hard and soft, largely abound. Oysters cover the banks where the water does not run too fast and the bottom is not sand; they are highly prized in all the markets. Those growing in Lynnhaven Bay, are by many considered to be the most delicious procurable in any part of the country. The birds are those common to the water as well as to the land; in the immediate vicinity of the fort only the tame kinds are to be met with. Gulls, apparently of many varieties, are constantly flying over the water.

The climate of Old Point is comparatively mild. The winters are open, and the thermometer, except in very rare cases, does not fall below 12° F. The duration of the cold periods seldom passes seventy-two hours, when the cold snaps give way and the mercury indicates an increase of temperature. The cold is, however, felt more perceptibly than in those regions where it is continuous. A continued frigid atmosphere to which the system becomes tempered is not only healthy but pleasant, but the fickleness of the Southern atmosphere in this section, is one great drawback to an otherwise almost faultless climate, and the system is far more susceptible to the influence of a decrease of temperature than it is in the more northern latitudes. There is but little snow here, and that which falls remains upon the ground but a short time.

The summers are long and hot. The summer heat commences in the early part of May, and continues until the latter part of September. During the months of June, July and August the heat is oppressive, and, were it not for the sea breeze, which commences to blow about 9 o'clock in the morning, would be almost unendurable. Within the walls of the fort the heat is much more oppressive than without them, as they serve to obstruct, in a great measure, the free range of the breeze which may be blowing. When on the beach or anywhere outside the temperature may be quite pleasant, within the inclosure it will be most oppressive. At night, however, the reverse holds, as a damp, murky atmosphere arises from the ground, imparting a chilly sensation with a feeling of moisture. There is, at night, a difference of two or three degrees in the temperature inside and outside of the fort.

During the winter season too, the temperature lowers within the walls, and the ground is much damper than when it is exposed to the unrestrained influence of wind and sun. The mean annual temperature of 1867 was 58.19°F. warmest day of the year was July 6. when mercury indicated 90° F. The coldest day was January 19, when the mercury at 7 o'clock A. M., indicated 14° F. The mean annual temperature of 1868 was 58.30° F. The warmest day was July 15, when the mercury indicated 92° F. The coldest day was December 25, when the mercury at 7 o'clock A. M., indicated 19° F. The amount of rain wich fell in 1867 was 64.26 inches. The greatest monthly amount of rain during the year was in August, when 11.40 inches fell. The amount of rain which fell in 1868 was 44.41 inches. The greatest monthly amount of rain in 1868 was in July, when 6.94 inches fell. The barometer ranges from 29.25 inches to 30.60 inches, which are the extremes reached here, as indicated by the record of four years, and afford a criterion upon which to base a judgment of the variations of heat and cold to which the extremes of the climate extend. Frequently the spring is much later than in other climates, vegetation very often not commencing till late in April, though sometimes prior to this time there are warmer periods sufficiently long to cause a budding and incipient blossoming of the fruit trees, which are subsequently blighted by severe frost.

The prevaling winds of spring and summer are southeast and southwest; those of fall and winter, east, northeast, and northwest. The easterly winds are the severest in February and March, and with them come diseases of the throat and lungs to both adults and infants. With the latter croup is most common in February and early March, when the winds chilled by the icebergs on the banks, continue blowing from the northeast for several successive days.

Having thus given in a general way the facts attending a journey to Fort Monroe, and detailed some of the phases to be met with by the traveler we will in our next chapter conduct him through the Fort itself, and relate in minutiae the data relating thereto.

CHAPTER III.

Fort Monroe.

First among the fortresses which guard our Nation's coast,
Monroe in mighty grandeur stands; King of all the rest.
Laved on all sides by its moated waters' ceaseless flow,
Over crystal Chesapeake, a silent sentinel
It stands, Columbia's faithful guard, in whom she trusts secure.

Fort Monroe, the geographical position of which has been given, and whose geological formation has been treated of elsewhere, was projected, with others, to cover the interior navigation, between Chesapeake Bay and the Southern States; to secure the roadstead and point, serving as the connecting link between the middle and southern coast as a naval place of arms, whence that arm of the public may operate, in defence of commerce and the public establishments at Norfolk, and such as were contemplated in James River; also to prevent an enemy making a lodgement in the direction of Norfolk.

Various Boards, both Military and Naval, had made these points the subject-matter of reports, ever since the close of the war with Great Britain, which closed in 1815. Experiences in that struggle, having taught them the importance of proper sea-coast defences, the attention of the Government was called to the fact, and accordingly on the 18th of January, 1817, the Secretary of the Navy transmitted to the Senate, opinions of the Board for the selection of a site for a naval depot and defensive works on the Chesapeake Bay.

The Senate, by resolutions, dated respectively, Feby. 13th 1817, and April 20th, 1818, directed the President to cause the survey of Hampton Roads, and York River, together with some other localities, with a view of ascertaining the practicability of defending the same by fortifications. In pursuance of this instruction, Brigadier Generals Swift and Bernard, Colonels Armistead and McKee, of the Engineers, were appointed commissioners, to co-operate with Captains Warrington and Elliott of the Navy, for the purpose of examining and surveying Hampton Roads and York River, and reporting how far it was practicable to defend said Roads and river, by fortifications.

The reports of the Boards were made in 1819 and 1820, and were voluminous and exhaustive, and embraced the inception of the present system of sea-coast defenses of the United States.

It is said to be traditional in the records of the Engineer Department, that Fort Monroe was planned by Gen. Simon Bernard, of the U. S. Engineers, formerly an officer under Napoleon I. in the Imperial Army of France. The drawings were made by Captain W. T. Poussin, of the Topographical Engineers, and Acting Aid to Gen. Bernard. In a report of a Board of Officers, on the subject of Military defenses, May 10th, 1840, an apology is made for its magnitude.

Materials having been accumulated at Old Point Comfort, Va., during the fall and winter of 1818, the construction of the Fort was actually commenced in March 1819, under Major Chas. Gratiot, Corps of Engineers ; and from 1822, until February 1824, all able-bodied soldiers, serving on the Atlantic coast, who were sentenced by Courts-Martial to hard labor, for periods exceeding six months, were employed on the work.

It was named "Fort Monroe," in honor of James Monroe

who was the President of the United States, when its construction was commenced. The first appropriation bill, in which the Fort is specifically mentioned, is that of March, 1821. Previous to this date appropriations had been made in general, without designating particular works.

The Post was first occupied by Battery "G," 3rd U. S. Artillery, June 1823, Captain M. P. Lomax, commanding. In February 1824, the Garrison was increased by Batteries "C," "D," and "I," 4th Artillery, Captain B. K. Pierce, 4th Artillery, assuming command. About this time the Artillery School, then known as "The Artillery School of Practice," was established, and is now in existence, known as the "United States Artillery School." The School has, however, been temporarily discontinued, at various times, when special exigencies, demanded the services of the troops elsewhere.

During the Civil War, 1861-5, the Post was garrisoned by one regiment of Heavy Artillery, 1800 men. Several expeditions have used this Post for a rendezvous and starting point. Gen. Sherman's expedition to South Carolina, sailed from this Point, Oct. 28th, 1861. Gen. Burnside's expedition to North Carolina, also sailed in January 1862. General Butler's expedition to Hatteras Inlet, in August 1861, and to Fort Fisher in December 1864, also had this place for their starting point. General Terry's expedition in January 1865, was fitted out at Fort Monroe. The Post was used as a base of supplies for the Army and Navy, operating on the line of the James River, and also along the coasts of North and South Carolina, during the entire period of the War.

Major Gen. Benj. F. Butler, commanded the Military Department of which Fort Monroe was the Headquarters, from May 22nd, 1861, to Aug. 17th 1861. He was succeeded by Major Gen. John E. Wool; who was followed, June 2nd, 1862, by Major Gen. John A. Dix, who commanded until July 18th,

1863; then followed Major Gen. John G. Foster to Nov. 11th 1863; Major Gen. B. F. Butler to Dec. 24th 1864, and Major Gen. E. O. C. Ord, to April 1865.

The Post then became the Headquarters of the 5th Regiment of Artillery, until Nov. 13th, 1867, when the Artillery School was again established, brevet Major Gen. Wm. F. Barry commanding, under whose able management, the School flourished, until March, 1877, when he was succeeded by brevet Major Gen. Geo. W. Getty, who retained command of the Post, until the fall of 1883, when he retired from the Army, and was succeeded by brevet Major Gen. John C. Tidball, the present commandant.

It may be interesting to note that the land included in the area of Fort Monroe, 252 acres, was ceded to the United States by the State of Virginia, March 1st, 1821, and conveyed to the former, by deed from the Governor, recorded in the Court of Elizabeth City County, Dec. 12th 1838. The records of Elizabeth City County were destroyed by fire, at the burning of Hampton, during the Rebellion, 1861-5. The title, however, is indisputable.

Mill Creek Bridge, which connects Old Point with the mainland, was deeded to the United States, by the Hampton River and Mill Creek Toll Bridge Company, Nov. 15th, 1838. About 14 acres of land, on the right bank of Mill Creek, opposite Fort Monroe, were conveyed to the United States by J. A. Bradford, Feb. 12th 1844. The Hygeia Hotel was first authorized June 25th 1868, and several times grants and privileges have been made, until it has reached its present mammoth proportions. Wm. H. Kimberly's Storehouse, authorized, March 16th, 1868. Adams Express Company Office, January 26th, 1880. Roman Catholic Chapel, June 8th, 1860. Ice House and Billiard Hall of Wm. Baulch, authorized February 26th, 1879.

The Fort is built in the shape of an irregular hexagon, five sides of which are nearly equal; the southeast front being as long as any of the other two. Each side has what is called a curtain, in other words, that part of the rampart or parapet, between the projecting portions, or bastions. These are so arranged that a fire from the salient angle, will protect the water front, in conjunction with the fire from the curtain, and the corner angles of each bastion, producing a cross fire, will protect the fosse, which surrounds the fort on all sides.

It has an average depth of about 8 feet, and is bricked for about one-third of the distance from the foundation walls, for the purpose of preventing the tide water from washing them away. A main sewer has been lately built running through the entire length of the Fort, and automatic flood gates placed on the north and east side of the moat, closing when the tide begins to ebb, and allowing no outlet for it, except through the sewer, is supposed to be powerful enough to carry off all the refuse matter of the Garrison. Branch sewers to each Officer's quarters, and from the Barracks, give a perfect network of drains, and form an admirable system of sewerage, and, when perfected, will contribute, in no small degree to the health of the Garrison. The sewer empties into the channel in Mill Creek.

The Moat is bridged at the three principal entrances of the Fort, termed the North, East, and West or Main Sally ports, and at the south-west, is a small bridge leading to what is termed the Postern Gate.

The area included within the counter-scarp or outside wall of the ditch, is 80 acres, and the remaining 252 acres include the grave yard, redoubt, and the rest of the reservation, extending to Mill Creek. Entering by the Main Gate, from the road leading from the Wharf, the first objects which attract our attention are the Guard Rooms, of which there are two.

One used for the confinement of prisoners, and the other for the use of the Guard. They are provided with bunks, gun-racks and all that go to make the necessary provisions for the sentries while on duty as sentinels. There are also four ordinary cells connected with one, and a dark cell connected with the other room. Besides these rooms, there are still two others, one of which is used by the Officer of the Guard, and in his absence, by the Non-commissioned Officers. The other is used for a tool room, although both, should any exigency demand it, are capable of being used as Guard rooms.

We pass the sentry, who, patrolling his beat, either at a "right shoulder arms" or, "support," gives no intimation either by word or look, that he is aware of our presence, unless we unwittingly trespass, or disobey his orders, when he will quickly inform us of the fact, and we see on our right a two story frame building, the second story of which is a photograph gallery.

Here are prepared views from different stand points, of the Fort, photographic maps of surveying tours, and, when desired, photographs of any person can be taken. Each Officer passing a term of two years at the School, goes under instruction in this branch, and all the accompaniments of a first class Gallery are to be found here. The advances lately made in Photography, whereby instaneous impressions can be taken, is availed of, and the liberality which furnishes first class instruments, and all their accompanying pharaphernalia, contributes in no small degree to the prosperity and usefulness of the School. It is amusing to see a picture of the Battalion in "double time," for instance, with one foot raised in the air, or a skirmish-line with a soldier with his foot just ready to be planted, but his "physog" taken just at that moment, leaving him in that position. However, they are specimens of the advanced stage of the Science, and show how well and ably.

the discipline and the usefulness of the School is preserved and enlarged, and made to tell in the instruction of the future guides of the Nation in Military matters.

The lower floor of this building is used for an Officers' Instruction Room, also for the storing of the Surveying Instruments when not in use. Just across from, and facing this building, is another frame structure. This is the Officers' Library. Here may be found valuable works on Military subjects in our own and other languages. Maps, records of the late war, important data on almost any subject pertaining to arms, can here be found grouped, together with histories of various descriptions, encyclopædias, biographies, the standard magazines of the day, pictorial histories of the Rebellion, and, in fact, any and all the works which go to make up a well assorted Military Library, of reference, interest, and instruction.

As we leave this building, we see a drab-colored brick structure, which lay on our left as we we entered the fort, which is the Post Hospital. The lower floor is the Dispensary, which contains a judicious and abundant selection of drugs and medicines, and the second and third stories, containing Wards for the sick. Here "Uncle Sam's boys," when they become disabled or temporarily ill, can be taken care of, and every arrangement made for their interest. Thanks to the salubrity and healthfulness of the climate, the health of the Garrison generally is good, and the services of the Surgeon, are not often called for severe cases. A Surgeon and Assistant Surgeon, both residing within the Garrison, render medical aid, when called upon.

After having looked at the Hospital, until our curiosity is satisfied, and passed the Matron's, quarters which with the Hospital Kitchen lie on the left and rear of it, we will next visit a small brick building in close proximity, which contains the Enlisted Mens' Library and Instruction Rooms. Here may be found between 3000 and 4000 of the leading Novels of the day, some in the Seaside, Lakeside, and Lovell's Library, but the majority of them, bound. All the leading dailies, tri-weeklis and weeklies, in the newspaper world, will be found on its tables, while Harper's, Frank Leslie, The Century, and other magazines of the highest literary merit, regale the lovers of fine reading, of whom there are quite a number. The Library is open from fatigue call in the morning, which is from 6.30 to 7.30 and 7.45 according to the Season, until 12 M., and from 1.00 P. M. until first signal for parade, about half an hour before sundown. The Officers' Library, termed, "The Artillery School Library," is open from 8 A. M., until 12 M., and from 1.00 P. M. until first signal for parade.

Looming in the foreground as we leave this building, are the Barracks, a fine two story brick structure, on the wings, and three stories, in the centre building. These are the quarters for the Enlisted men, and more commodious and more perfectly arranged quarters, few, if any other posts, can boast. A veranda, running the full length of each wing, on both first and second floors, adds a finish to the front of the structure, as well as affording a pleasant place for the soldiers to sit. The Barracks contain six sets of Company Quarters, each, a fac-simile of the rest. On the lower floor are the Office, Store Room, 1st Sergeant's Room, Wash and Bath Rooms, and Day Room, on one side of the Hall, and Dining Room, Kitchen, Sleeping Room for the Cooks, and Store Room for the rations, on the other side.

On the second floor, to which we ascend by an iron staircase are two dormitories, each capable of accommodating 30 men comfortably, and should necessity require it, more could be crowded in. They are provided with iron bunks, and cotton mattresses and pillows. Shelves ranging round the rooms afford ample accommodations for the clothing, while a plentiful sprinkling of windows, makes the barrack-room light and cheerful.

The building is heated throughout by steam, two registers being placed in each dormitory, two in each hallway on the first floor, one in the Office, Day Room, 1st Sergeant's Room Wash and Bath Rooms, and they keep the Quarters comfortably heated with a good head of steam on. The steam is supplied from the Engine House, a brick building, lying immediately in rear of the Quarters. A verandah, on the second floor, runs the entire length of both wings in rear. Both salt and fresh water are supplied to the Barracks, by means of the New Water Works, to be completed during the coming Summer. The Main Building contains on the ground floor, on one side of the sally-port, one long room, which is utilized as the Post Barber Shop, and on the other side two stair cases leading to the Court Martial Room on the second floor, from the front of the building, and the other, from the rear, leading to what is termed the Tank Room ; this contains three large zinc tanks, from which a supply of fresh water is obtained for the Bath Rooms and Kitchen.

On the third floor of this building is the Amusement Hall, or "Hop Room," as it is generally termed, where hops, theatrical performances, and, in fact, amusements of all kind were held, until recently. Not long since its use was interdicted, the floor being condemned as weak, and too unsafe to risk dancing on it.

The New Water Works, but partially completed at present, are intended to supply the Garrison with both salt and fresh water. The mains for both are laid one on top of the other. Fire plugs at convenient distances, will enable the water to be thrown high enough to cover the top of the highest structure in the Fort, and so will prove an invaluable auxiliary in case of fire. The water will be procured from the Government farm, at what is known as "Slabtown." The pipes for the same are laid across Mill Creek, and the water will be drawn from the well by a suction pump.

The Reservoir will be placed over the North Gate, and will have a capacity of about 50,000 gallons. The water will have a fall of about 60 feet.

Leaving the Main Building, and taking the main walk, we see on our left the Ordnance Store House, a two story brick building, containing every species of Ordnance Stores, in use in the Artillery. The lower floor is used also, for storing the Hotchkiss and Gatling guns, of which there are fine specimens at the Post. Next we see two drab colored buildings, called "Knox Row," so named by the Commandant at the time of their erection, the late Gen. Wm. F. Barry, in honor of the Sec'y of War, Hon. Henry Knox. They are residences of Officers, having passed which, we come to the Commandant's dwelling house. This is a very fine structure, being approached by a broad flight of steps from both front and rear. Ample grounds surround the dwelling, while a garden and Green House, add their attractive features to its grace and beauty. A garden, in charge of a soldier, who spends his time in furthering the growth of the ornamental and useful in the vegetable and botanical world, lies in rear of the dwelling. It is a very pleasant residence.

Walking a few steps further we come to the Headquarters of the United States Artillery School. These are very ordinary frame structures, erected by Gen. Butler during the War. The first building contains the Adjutant's, Sergeant Major's and Printing Office. The second contains the Commandant's Office. The Printing Office well repays a visit, as here may be seen in their different stages the printing and binding of a great many of the text-books, used in the School: all the Lithographing of the School is also done here, which with its sister science Photography, has done so much for, and occupies such a prominent place in Military Science of the day.

For maps, plates for text-books, and in fact everywhere it can be utilized to advantage, lithography is made use of, and, be it spoken to the credit of the rank and file of the Army, all the work is performed by Enlisted Men. The specimens furnished of their skill, proving them, able to cope in their several departments, with mechanics at large in the world. Until recently a very lively little sheet, termed, " Fort Monroe Gazette," a five column four page paper, published semi-monthly, was issued from this same office, and had quite a large circulation in the neighborhood ; the entire publishing and editorial force of which, was composed of Enlisted Men.

Leaving Headquarters, and continuing our promenade, we pass a double brick house, with beautiful verandas running in front of both first and second floors. These dwellings were formerly the property of the Ordnance Department, but when the Arsenal was removed entirely outside of the Fort, these buildings were turned over to the Post, and are now used as Officers' Quarters.

Passing these, our next object of interest is the Post Chapel. " Church of the Centurion." It is a frame building 70x27 feet inside, besides a recess chancel 19x16 feet on one end, and a porch 10x9 feet on the other end. It was erected after plans made by the late Richard Upjohn, a church architect in New York City. It was commenced in 1857, and finished in 1858. The most active part in its erection, was taken by Lieut. McAllister of the Ordnance ; now Colonel. The Colonel intended to show by this action, his recognition of the Divine mercy toward him in preserving his life in an explosion in a laboratory, in which he and two other Officers, were at work. They were killed and his own life preserved.

The chapel was at first furnished with rough pine benches, and neither chancel nor chapel furniture, expressed aught of the taste of the worshipers, or was in consistency with the idea which must always make itself felt in an appreciative mind, that a house dedicated to the worship of God, should express, in all its appointments, the reverence and sanctity felt by its communicants, and their acknowledgement of the same, by their liberality in its appropriate adornment. In consistency with this sentiment, the present chaplain, Rev. Osgood E. Herrick, U. S. A. in conjunction with his estimable wife, assisted by the ladies of the church, inaugurated Fairs, which were held at the Hygeia Hotel, and raised subscriptions by this means, and others of a like character, for the purpose of furnishing in a proper manner, our Post Chapel.

Many articles of ornament and use were manufactured, and among them all, none, perhaps, attracted more attention, or met with a quicker sale, than negro nurses in miniature, with an infant in their arms, negro men-of-war sailors, and cotton pickers, most of these being manufactured by Mrs. Herrick herself. The result speaks for itself, in the improved appearance of the Chapel to-day.

Handsome black walnut pews, take the place of the unsightly pine benches. Magnificent stained glass windows, eight of them memorial, one, dedicated to the late Gen. W. F. Barry, being particularly worthy of mention, take the place of the old ones. A handsome carpet covering the floor, and rich chancel furniture, combine to make this little house of worship, a model of neatness and elegance. A beautifully built, and sweetly toned Organ, from the firm of Jardine & Sons of New York, furnishes appropriate music, and charms all who hear it. The Choir of the chapel is composed entirely of enlisted men, and reflects credit alike upon the command and themselves, by their endeavors to aid in the service. Services are held every Sabbath at 10.45 A. M., and Evening service, at different hours, from 3 to 5.30 P. M., varying with the season.

Leaving this delightful little spot, which we are loath to do, and continuing our journey on foot, we come to two more dwelling houses on our right, the residences of the Post Chaplain and Assistant Surgeon. Then comes a row of buildings, which were named, when first built, "The Tuileries," on account it is supposed, of their being the handsomest buildings in the Fort at the time. Immediately in rear of these quarters, is a small alley-way running between them and two other Officers' quarters, and dubbed, in the parlance of the Garrison "Ghost Alley." Why this name, is involved in mystery. The most plausible explanation perhaps, is, that until lately, no lights were placed here, and as darkness invariably associates itself with ghosts and ghost stories, it is a natural supposition, that it thus arose. Lights have been recently placed at each end, and the significance of the name, if it ever possessed any, will doubtless pass away.

We have now reached the southwest postern gate commonly called "No. 2." This entrance is largely used by the guests of the Hygeia Hotel, and the Officers of the Garrison. It is closed to Enlisted Men and strangers (except Officers' guests) after "Retreat," which is at sunset. Commencing at "No. 2," we have a line of casemated quarters; they are casemates for guns which would form the Flank Defence of the Fort, and have been ceiled and floored, and made into comfortable and convenient dwellings. In case of necessity, however, they could be quickly metamorphosed into an armed battery, whence the iron mouthed "dogs of war," could belch forth their iron hail, carrying destruction and ruin to an opposing enemy. They are termed respectively, First, Second and Third Fronts. First and Second Fronts, are used by the Officers, while Third Front is used principally by enlisted men. First Front must ever be memorable, in the history of Fort Monroe, since it was the scene of the incarceration of Jefferson & Davis, President of the Southern Confederacy. "On the 19th, of May, 1865, the *William P. Clyde*, dropped anchor in Hampton Roads, and the news quickly spread on shore, that she had on board, several State prisoners, viz., Jefferson Davis, President of the Confederacy and his family ; Alexander H. Stephens, Vice-president; John N. Reagan, Postmaster General ; Clement C. Clay, and several others."

"What will they do with him?" "When will they bring him ashore?" "Guess they'll take him to Washington and hang him by Military Commission?" "Guess you're a jackass; they can't hang him unless they hang all." "Jackass yourself; the papers say he was with the assassins in killing Lincoln." "Who are the other chaps with him?" "Will they keep him in the woman's toggery he had on when they caught him?" "Guess there's no truth in that." "It's just as true as preaching—all the papers say so." "They'll hang Clem Clay sure." Such was a specimen of the conversation going on, on shore, concerning those on board the *Clyde*.

"Blacksmiths and carpenters, had been busy fitting up Casemates Nos. 2 and 4, first front, near the Postern Gate, for the reception of the prisoners. They were partitioned off, into regular cells, by bricklayers ; heavy iron bars were placed across the external embrasures, and windows opening on the interior; and the cells for the prisoners were partitioned off into two apartments, that next to the embrasure, being intended for the captives, while the room or cell opening on the interior of the fort, was intended for their guard."

"On the morning of the 21st of May, some of the minor

State prisoners on board the *Clyde*, the Confederate General Wheeler and his staff, were placed on board the *Maumee*, which then steamed for Fort Warren in Boston Harbor, while Alexander H. Stephens, ex-Postmaster Reagan, and some others were soon after transferred on board the gunboat *Tuscarora*, which immediately started off to Fort Delaware, as was presumed."

"Intense excitement, on shore and in the neighboring vessels, accompanied all these changes; but Major General Halleck, who had come down some days before to superintend the arrangements, would make no sign, and speculation consequently ran higher and higher every moment, as to whether the chief prisoner of all was destined to remain at the fort, or be transferred elsewhere in custody without halting."

Speculation was rife concerning the matter, but all conjectures were at last put to rest, by the arrival of Major General Miles, in a special steamer from Baltimore, that officer having been assigned to the command of the Fort, Colonel Roberts, the Commandant, having been relieved. This was on the afternoon of May 22d. As soon as the officer arrived, a chain of sentinels was posted, to keep back the crowd, from the Engineers Landing to the Postern Gate. These arrangements all proved that the object of all these details, the prisoner, for whose appearance all the crowd were on the *qui vive*, was about to be landed.

The parting on board the *Clyde*, between Mr. Davis and his family, was affecting in the extreme, the ladies weeping very bitterly, as Messrs. Clay and Davis were handed over the ship's side, into the boat which was to convey them on shore. After landing, the procession was formed, Major General Halleck, and the Hon. Charles A. Dana, Assistant Secretary of War, inspecting the same. Col. Pritchard, of the Michigan cavalry, who effected the capture, being in command of the

Guard, while passing from the *Clyde* to the Fort. General Miles led the procession, arm-in-arm with Mr. Davis, who was dressed in a plain Confederate grey suit and slouched hat, looking very much wasted and haggard.

Thus they passed through files of "Uncle Sam's boys," from the landing place, to the Postern Gate. When they arrived at their destination, Mr. Davis was shown into No. 2 Casemate, and Mr. Clay, into No. 4. Guards were placed in the cells immediately contiguous thereto, Nos. 1, 3 and 5. They were ushered in, and the doors clanged behind them, and thus was rung the final knell, of those who had indulged in such high hopes, respecting one of the most stupendous struggles of modern times, but whose star had set in darkness and despair.

General Miles showed Mr. Davis into his cell, and the two doors leading thereinto being closed, Mr. Davis surveyed the premises for a few moments, and then placing his hands on his knees, having previously seated himself in a chair, looked intently at one of the sentinels pacing up and down, and bluntly asked: "Which way does the embrasure face?" No answer was made to this query. The question was repeated. But again naught but silence was his answer, broken only by the footfalls of his guards, both within and without his cell. He then addressed the other sentry with the same words, eliciting no response whatever. "Well," said Mr. Davis, throwing up his hands and breaking into a bitter laugh. "I wish my men could have been taught your discipline!" Then rising from his chair, he paced his cell back and forth, ever and anon, looking from the embrasure, at the sentry on the opposite side of the moat, and then at his two silent companions.

Who shall tell the cause of his sardonic mirth, for he was seldom known to indulge in laughter. Was he living in retrospect the days when, under President Pierce, his approach to the Fort was signalized by the roar of guns from whose embrasures he now looked forth a prisoner of War? Was not his question pregnant with meaning? "Which way does the embrasure face?" "To what point of the compass is my gaze directed?" "Am I looking toward the scenes of my late ambitious hopes, the theatre of War, from whose flames I have marched to disaster and imprisonment, or am I looking Northward, where throned in power, and representing the august majesty of the law, my enemies sit in state?" That day which shall reveal all events, only can tell.

The next morning, however, was to witness the most severe trial to which the proud spirit of the prisoner had yet been put. Perhaps no one occupying so lofty a position, has ever been subject to so severe an ordeal in modern times. On May 23rd, Jefferson Davis was shackled. While this event was transpiring at Fort Monroe, another of a different character, but intimately connected with the history of the prisoner, was being enacted at Washington. The armies of the the Potomac, of Tennessee, and Georgia, were preparing for that grand review, in which two hundred thousand battle scarred and war bronzed veterans, were to pass in Grand Review before the President, and lay down their arms at the feet of the Civil Authority, and retire to the avocations of private life, which some of them left four years before at their country's call.

On that morning, Capt. J. E. Titlow, of the 3rd Pennsylvania Artillery, Officer of the Day, entered the cell, accompanied by the post blacksmith and assistant, the latter carrying the shackles in his hands, whose chains clanked harshly together. Mr. Davis having passed a very restless night, was reclining on his couch, his food furnished him the previous day, remaining untouched beside him.

As they entered Mr. Davis arose. "Well," said he. "I have a very unpleasant duty to perform, Sir," said Captain Titlow, and as he spoke, the blacksmith came forward with the shackles. As soon as the prisoner realized the situation, his face flushed for a moment, and then became pale and rigid as death. He drew his figure up to its full height, apparently dumbfounded with indignation, and then he seemed to shrink in terror from such a trying ordeal. He said: — "My God! You cannot have been sent to iron me?" "Such are my orders, Sir," replied the officer, and he signified to the blacksmith, that he was awaiting the performance of his duty.

"The fetters were of heavy iron, about five-eighths of an inch in thickness, and connected together by a chain of like weight." They are now believed to be in the possession of General Miles.

"This is too monstrous," groaned the prisoner, "I demand, Captain, that you let me see the Commanding Officer. Can he pretend that such shackles are required, to secure the safe custody of a weak old man, so guarded, and in such a fort as this?"

"It could serve no purpose," replied Captain Titlow, his orders are from Washington."

"But he can telegraph," said Mr. Davis quickly; "there must be some mistake. No such outrage as you threaten, is on record in the history of nations. Beg him to telegraph, and delay until he answers."

"My orders are peremptory," said the officer, and admit of no delay. For your sake, let me advise you to submit with patience. As a soldier, Mr Davis, you know I must execute orders."

"These are not orders from a soldier," shouted the prisoner, "they are the orders of a jailor, for a hangman, which no soldier wearing a sword should accept! I tell you the world will ring with this disgrace. The war is over, the South is conquered; I have no longer any country but America, and it is for the honor of America, as for my own honor and life, that I plead against this degradation. Kill me! Kill me!" he cried, "rather than inflict on me and my people through me, this insult worse than death."

"Do your duty, blacksmith," said Captain Titlow, walking away, as if unwilling to witness such a painful ceremony. "It only gives increased pain on both sides, to protract this interview."

The blacksmith, in obedience to his orders, attempted to obey them, and seeing one foot of the prisoner resting upon a chair near his bed, he tried to slip one of the shackles on. With a strength born of frenzy, and an amount of physical power wholly unlooked for, Mr. Davis seized the blacksmith, and hurled him half-way across the room.

Captain Titlow turning at this juncture, and seeing Mr. Davis still bent on further resistance, remonstrated with him, and besought him, for his own sake, not to protract matters, which must eventually terminate in his own discomfiture. "Why compel me, to add the further indignity," said he "of personal violence to the necessity of being ironed."

"I am a prisoner of War," said Mr. Davis, "I have been a soldier in the army of America, and know how to die. Only kill me, and my last breath shall be a blessing on your head. But while I have life and strength to resist, for myself and for my people, this thing shall not be done."

The Captain then called for a sergeant and a file of soldiers, and the sergeant attempted to seize the prisoner. Thereupon Mr. Davis attempted to wrest his musket from him, when he was immediately seized by the four men, and when he arose he was manacled. He dropped his feet to the floor, and as the clank of the chain first sounded on his ears, he burst into a violent fit of weeping, and covering his face with his hands, he kept continually repeating : — "Oh, the shame ! The shame !"

Mr. Davis, in speaking afterwards, said he was never tempted, or at least, never sought his own life but once, and that was when he grasped the sergeant's musket, and he said he did it, hoping the men would bury their bayonets in him.

For three days, the prisoner ate scarcely anything, and the fare of the soldiers not agreeing with him, his medical attendant, brevet Lieut. Col. John H. Craven, recommended a light diet, which was granted him, and he supped on the evening of May 26th, on toast and tea, for which he seemed very grateful. The wearing of his shackles having a very deleterious effect, the Surgeon recommended their removal, and Gen. Miles, on Sunday May 28th, ordered their removal.

During his confinement, Mr. Davis held repeated conversations with his Surgeon, on various subjects, and freely expressed his views in regard to the War, and also as to some acts with which he was charged, such as the repudiation of the Mississippi bonds, which he emphatically denied.

The health of the prisoner fluctuated considerably, until the 14th of August, when he was attacked, with incipient erysipelas, and a carbuncle on his thigh, which continued to grow worse until September 1st, when Col. Craven, attributing the cause of the disease to the damp casemate, wrote a letter to Gen. Miles, requesting his removal to more comfortable quarters. The rooms in the second story of the south end of Carroll Hall, were selected as the place best suited for the purpose.

This building had been long used as officers' quarters, and nearly every officer of the old army was quartered here, after leaving West Point. Rumor hath it, that both Grant and Sherman occupied these same rooms, before the imprisonment of Mr. Davis there.

Two rooms were used, as in the casemate prison.— Through a grated door connecting the two rooms, a constant view of the inner room could be obtained, and his guard, consisting of a Lieutenant and two soldiers, were stationed in the outer room, and kept a vigilant watch over his every movement, to prevent any attempt at suicide. Opposite the grated door was a fireplace. On the right was a heavily grated window, and a sentry continually paced up and down in front of it. Opposite this window was a door leading into the corridor, and here a sliding panel had been fixed, and the door heavily barred, and a sentry continually kept his face pressed there, to report the slightest effort on the part of the prisoner to attempt self destruction. The piazza was extended, and a flight of steps placed there, so that the prisoner could mount the ramparts, without descending to the ground floor.

On October 5th he removed to Carroll Hall, and was allowed every day to walk for an hour on the ramparts. Mr. Davis suffered much inconvenience, from the morbid curiosity of those, who, visiting the Fort seemed, to regard him as a novelty, at which they were at perfect liberty to gaze, and speculate concerning. Mr. Davis tried to rebuke this lack of good breeding, by turning abruptly to his cell, but without avail. After being confined at Carroll Hall about eight months, under the closest surveillance, not being allowed to walk on the ramparts, without the Officer of the Day, Sergeant of the Guard, and a file of the Guard, in attendance, the prisoner was granted a parole, which allowed him the limits of the Garrison. His family having arrived, in the meantime, three casemates in Second Front, immediately facing the Engine House, were occupied by him and his loved ones. He was allowed the liberty of the Fort, but orders were issued to the effect, that if he attempted to pass out at any of the entrances, to halt him, and if he refused to obey, to shoot him on the spot. Things remained in this condition, concerning Mr. Davis, until the fall of 1866, when he was taken to Richmond, and brought before the United States District Court, on a charge of treason.

He was released on bail, three prominent Northern men, Horace Greely being one, becoming his bondsmen. The matter was never brought to trial, and the affair was quashed. Mr. Davis refused to take the "Iron Clad Oath" of allegiance, and was disfranchised, and to-day he stands, an anomaly in the history of the world, a man without a country, and without a precedent.

He is now living in Mississippi, and recently, just previous to the opening of the New Orleans Exposition, while transporting the old "Independence Bell," from Philadelphia to New Orleans, those having it in charge, stopped at Mr. Davis's place of residence, and he delivered quite a speech. appropriate to the subject and occasion.

Thus we leave him. In his moments of reverie, when he dwells upon the pictures of the past, if remorse mingles with his retrospect, who would wonder? His errors in judgment, or his intentional treason, it is not our province, to either condone or condemn. To his own conscience, and his God, must be left the solving of the problem.

Carroll Hall, the place of his imprisonment, is approached qy a brick walk, branching off from the walk leading past the Hospital, and is used, exclusively, for Officers' quarters.

Returning to first front, and continuing our tour of sightseeing, at its terminus, we see the Officers' Club Room, fitted up for the accommodation and pleasure of the Officers of the Post. Here may be found Billiard and Pool Tables, a fine Bar, and all the accompaniments of a first-class Club Room. Second front, next greets us, and when we arrive at its end, we see the Post Bakery, fitted up and occupying two casemates. Here all the bread consumed by the Garrison, is made by enlisted men, and many citizens avail themselves of the privilege granted them, and purchase their bread here also. Those who have partaken of it, can testify to its good quality.

On the other side of the "ramps," is the "Sutler Store," which is presided over by Wm. Baulch, Post Trader, whose able management, provides the Enlisted Men of the Garrison, with everything which a soldier can possibly need, from "boots to hat."

Third front, is the next object we meet, which is flanked at each end, by two small magazines. There are also two small magazines at each end of second front, all about the same size. The largest magazine in the Garrison, lies on the left of Carroll Hall, and one other is situated in the group of buildings known as the Post "Commissary." These buildings were formerly the property of the Ordnance Department, but when the Arsenal was removed outside of the Fort, these were turned over to the Post, with the rest of the buildings belonging to the same Department, and have since been used for the purpose above specified. They are situated in the northeastern portion of the Fort, and lie on the right of the North Gate.

During our promenade, we have noticed several roadways, leading from the Main road to the ramparts. The majority of these are built up what is termed, the "interior slope," while two others, the one at the Sutler Store, and the other leading from the main road ,between First and Second fronts, to the flag staff, stand out in bold relief, with their capstones arranged as steps. These are so built, to break the joints of the masonry, which would be weakened, if built in any other manner. These roadways are termed "ramps," and lead from the road to what is termed the *terreplein*, upon which the guns are mounted.

We will ascend the one leading from the "Sutler Store," and we find ourselves in the South Bastion, which is the central one on the southeast side of the Fort; this curtain, as has already been stated, being longer than any other. Here will be found mounted, one 15" Centre Pintle Gun, improved pattern, with compressed air cylinders; the old model gun of this calibre, is run "in battery," and "from battery," by means of handspikes, whereas, in the new model, the gun, when the axle is unkeyed, will run "in battery" automatically.

Turning to our left we come to what is termed the Southeast Bastion, where are mounted Parrott Guns and one 15" Centre Pintle of the "old model," which was the first ever manufactured, and it was named the "Lincoln Gun," after President Lincoln. Here will be found 8" "Converted Rifles," so called because they are made by boring out ordinary 10" Smooth Bore guns and inserting a double lining tube of coiled wrought-iron. The tube is secured from working out by a muzzle collar, screwed in at the face of the piece, and from turning, by a steelpin tapped through the casing.

While taking our promenade on the *terreplein*, we have noticed a large majority of the unused platforms, are of brick, with stone facings. These were built in the days of the old wooden carriages, and are now useless. In time they will superseded by platforms suited for heavy guns. Immediately in rear of the Commissary Buildings, is the Northeast Bastion.

At the other end of the curtain, is the Northwest Bastion, which lies immediately in rear, of Carroll Hall. Nothing of importance meets the eye between this bastion and the next one, which is the Southwest Bastion. The platforms for guns, commence from this point to be numbered, the platform for the C. P. 15″ being No. 1.

The only Bastion now remaining, is the Flag-staff Bastion, from which the morning and evening gun is fired.

From the *terreplein*, we will ascend to the crest of the ramparts themselves, and enjoy an unobstructed view of the Roads and Bay. From the crest to the scarp wall, is termed the "exterior slope," while from the *terreplein* to the road, is named the "interior slope." The outside wall of the ditch is termed the counter-scarp.

Looking from the ramparts to the other side of the moat, we notice it is divided into three parts, viz., from the southern end of the Water Battery to the Northwest Bastion, an easy slope extends, which is termed the glacis, and is protected, by the guns from the fort proper. Then commences, what is termed, the "Covered Way," a wall, a little more than breast high, which is intended as a cover and protection for troops, when, falling back from the outworks, they seek the protection of the fort, and extends to the northern end of the Water Battery. The Water Battery itself, forms the third part, and we will now describe it.

Taking our way through the East Gate, immediately in front of the Commandant's dwelling, we enter the Water Battery,

The next point of interest, is the "Place of Arms," a recess, in which troops could be sheltered and secreted, to repel an attack form land forces, and, with the Redoubt, from the outworks of the Fort.

On the Parade ground of the Fort, we have, to the right of the Main Walk, as we face Headquarters, the Siege Battery Park. It contains Siege Guns and a Siege Howitzer.

On the left of the Main Walk, we have the Light Battery Park, which contains four 3 inch Rifles, and two brass twelve pounders or Napoleon guns. In the rear of the pieces themselves, between them and their caissons, is a Mortar Battery, consisting of four 8″ Siege Mortars.

The 3-inch Rifle, was adopted in 1861. It is made of wrought iron, by wrapping boiler iron round an iron bar, so as to form a cylindrical mass, which is brought to a welding heat, and passed through rollers, so as to unite it solidly ; the trunnions are afterwards welded on, and the piece is bored and turned to its proper size and shape.

The Mitrailleur or Gatling guns, were adopted in 1868 ; they are made of steel, some of the smaller parts being brass. The twelve-pounder, or Napoleon gun, adopted in 1857, is still in use in the United States service, though abandoned by all other nations. It is cast in gun-metal, or bronze, which consists of ninety parts of copper and ten of tin, allowing a variation of one part more or less.

The charges are contained in cartridge-bags, made of woolen material, of sufficiently close texture to prevent the powder from sifting through, the size varying with the charge. Mitrailleur ammunition, is put up in metallic cases ; it is primed, fixed and ready for use.

Rifle projectiles are designated by the diameter of the bore of the piece in which they are used ; their shape is oblong ; they are not attached to their cartridge. Smooth-bore projectiles, are designated by the weight in pounds of the solid-shot of the same diameter ; their shape is spherical, with the exception of canister, which is cylindrical in form ; they are *fixed* or attached to their cartridges by wooden disks called *sabots*.

A projectile and its cartridge, constitute a *round of ammunition*. The projectiles used in light batteries, are *shell, case-shot, canister*, and *solid-shot*.

A *shell* is a hollow, cast-iron projectile, made strong enough to penetrate earthworks, wooden buildings, etc., without breaking; it is loaded with a bursting charge of rifle or musket powder, which gives great force to the fragments. Fire is communicated to the charge by means of a fuse, inserted in the hole by which the shell is loaded; it is divided into seconds, and the time of the explosion, is regulated accordingly.

A *case-shot* is a hollow, cast-iron projectile, filled with musket-balls, and with thinner walls than those of the shell. A tube is inserted in the fuse-hole, the balls are introduced, and melted sulphur or rosin is poured in to fill up the interstices, and keep the balls in position; after this has solidified, the tube is withdrawn, leaving a vacant space for the charge, which is only large enough to burst the case, and disperse the contents. Fire is communicated to the charge, in the same manner as prescribed for a shell.

A *canister* shot consists of a hollow cylinder, filled with cast-iron or lead balls, which vary in size and number with the calibre and kind of pieces; the cylinder is closed at the bottom by a thick cast-iron plate, and at the top by one of sheet-iron. A canister shot for the three-inch Rifle contains from one hundred to one hundred and fifty balls; that for the twelve-pounder, twenty-seven balls; the interstices between the balls are filled with sawdust. Canister shot for rifled guns, has an expanding metallic sabot or cuff.

A *solid-shot* is made of cast-iron.

There are four principal kinds of projectiles used with the

3-inch Rifle. viz., the *Hotchkiss*, the shell of which weighs 8.5 lbs., and requires a charge of 3 oz., of cannon powder; the case shot weighs 9 lbs., contains 24 balls, and requires a bursting charge of 1 oz. of cannon powder; the canister weighs 7.5 lbs., and the solid shot 10 lbs.; the *Ordnance* projectile, the shell of which weighs 7.5 lbs., requiring 10 oz. of powder to fill it; the case shot weighing 10.5 lbs., containing 49 balls with a bursting charge of 1 oz. of powder, and the canister weighing 10 lbs.; the *Absterdam* projectile, the shell of which weighs 10.5 lbs., and requires 8 oz., of powder to fill it; the case-shot weighing 11.62 lbs., containing 58 balls and requiring a bursting charge of 2 oz. of powder, and the solid shot weighing 9.5 lbs.; the *Eureka* projectile, the shell of which weighs 9 lbs. requiring 8 oz. of powder to fill it, and the case-shot weighing 11.6 lbs., containing 42 balls, and requiring a bursting charge of 1 oz. of powder. The shell for the Napoleon gun, weighs 9.52 lbs., and requires 8 oz. of powder to fill it; the case-shot weighs 12.17 lbs., contains 76 balls, and requires a bursting charge of 1 oz. of powder; the canister weighs 14.80 lbs., and the solid shot weighs 12.75 lbs.

Left of the Main Walk leading from the Barracks to the "Sutler Store," and just before reaching it, we see a triangular shaped piece of ground, which is termed "Trophy Park" and contains interesting souvenirs of Conwallis's surrender at Yorktown, in 1781. The three angles are occupied by three 10″ Siege Mortars, each flanked by triangular piles of Mortar Shells. In the centre of the Park is a brass Mortar, which was originally used for firing stone, by having them placed in a basket prepared for the purpose. Its use was long since abolished. Surrounding this, on all sides, are rows of 10″ Mortar Shells, and above these, a row of projectiles for the 8″ Rifle. The trophies consist of 3 Howitzers, manufactured respectively in 1829, 1740 and 1677: each having two handles, the handles of two of them being dolphins, and the third plain; two Siege pieces, manufactured respectively in 1759 and 1767 the first named bearing a Coat- of-Arms, and the following inscription;—"The Right Hon. George Sackville, Lt. General, and the rest, of the principal officers in His Majesty's Ordnance," and each having the dolphin handles, before referred to; two field pieces, one about 3 inches, and the other 4 inches, in diameter. In addition to the insciption already referred to, each trophy has the English Coat-of-Arms and the following:—"Surrendered at the Capitulation of Yorktown, Oct. 19th, 1781."

In addition to these, there is also a breech-loading Chinese gun, which was known in Chinese vernacular, as a "Breech-loading Wall Piece." It bears the following inscription in the Chinese language:—" 19th year, 2nd Moon, of the Chinese Emperor, King Hi. A. D. 1681." The gun also bears the names of high Military Officials, that of the Superintendent of Casting, two subordinate Superiors, and of the Master Workman. This gun was captured from the Coreans, by the U. S. Naval Squadron, commanded by Rear-Admiral Jno. Rogers, U. S. Navy, and was presented to the Museum of the " U. S. Artillery School," by Major Wallace F. Randolph, 5th U. S. Artillery.

We have completed our tour of the Fort, having exhausted the interesting features. Its Garrison is composed at present, of five batteries, "A" of the 3rd, "K" of the 2nd, "I" of the 4th, "C" of the 5th, and "G" of the 1st, Regiments of United States Artillery. Battery "A" is commanded by Capt. James Chester, Battery "K" is commanded by brevet Major John H. Calef, Battery "I" is commanded by brevet Major J. B. Campbell, Battery "C" is commanded by Capt. Chas.

Morris, and Battery "G," is commanded by Capt. James M. Ingalls.

The Staff of the Commandant brevet Brigadier-General Jno. C. Tidball is composed of the following officers, Major A. C. M. Pennington, 4th Artillery, Major Richard Lodor, 3rd Artillery, Surgeon Joseph C. Baily, Medical Department, Assistant Surgeon George S. Torney, Rev. Osgood E. Herrick, Post Chaplain, Captain Charles A. Booth, Post Quartermaster, and Captain Frank E. Nye, C. S. The Fort Monroe Arsenal is commanded by Lawrence S. Babbitt, Major of Ordnance.

The batteries are supposed to number 48 men strong, including the Non-commissioned Officers, of which there are 9 to each, 1st Sergeant, 4 duty Sergeants, and 4 Corporals. A daily detail is made, from Headquarters, of a pro rata proportion of each battery, for the Post Guard, which is mounted every morning, the signal being sounded at 8:30 A. M. It is a beautiful and interesting ceremony. These details are made on a basis derived from a daily report of each battery, termed "The Morning Report," which is signed by the Commanding Officer of the battery, and taken by the First Sergeant, who also signs it, to Headquarters. These books must be presented by 8 o'clock. A. M., and the details are then made by the Post Sergeant-Major for the next day.

Drill occurs in the afternoon of each day, except Saturday and Sunday, the signal being sounded at from 2:30 to 4:30 P. M., varying with the season. It lasts an hour and a half, and consits of Heavy Artillery, Light Artillery, and Battalion Drills and Target Practice with small arms. In the Summer season, all the Artillery Target Practice of the Post takes place, under the supervision of the Officers of the Class. Each of the Departments is under the supervision of an Instructor.

The Course of instruction comprises two years, so that every two years, a new class arrives at the Post. Two First and two Second Lieutenants, to each Battery, making lv.en in all, compose the Class. Sometimes an Infantry, Caval or Marine Officer, is numbered among them.

There is a Dress Parade every evening, except Saturday, sunset, Weekly Inspection every Sunday Morning, at 8:30 . M. by the Captains, and Monthly Inspection, by the Commanding Officer, on the last day of every month.

Having thus far conducted our readers, we will leave the hoping they have enjoyed the tour, and derived some usef information therefrom.

THE END.

www.ingramcontent.com/pod-product-compliance
Lightning Source LLC
Chambersburg PA
CBHW020149170426
43199CB00010B/950